"Not only does this book tell you what's really going on, but it even draws you a picture of it. Read, learn, act!"
— Jim Hightower, radio commentator and author of *Thieves in High Places* and *If the Gods Had Meant Us to Vote…*

"Thom Hartmann has done it again! He's like America's Civics Teacher, telling us everything we need to know about what democracy really is, and how to protect it when threats abound."
— Marianne Williamson, co-founder, Global Renaissance Alliance, and author of *Healing the Soul of America* and *Everyday Grace*

"An ambitious effort to explain everything that's wrong in and about America, how things got this way and what should be done about it, *We the People* is the product of a brilliant and principled thinker."
— Ted Rall, syndicated cartoonist and author of *2024* and *Gas War: The Truth Behind the American Occupation of Afghanistan*

"Whether he's writing about ADHD, corporations, or, now, the task of restoring democracy in America, Thom Hartmann has a gift for making complex subjects clear and accessible. This book can empower young and old to take responsibility for the future of our world."
— Eric Utne, Founder, *Utne magazine*

"There's nothing childish or 'cartoonish' about the ideas, strategies, and analysis in this brilliant book. It should be available everywhere as a quick, accurate primer on what has gone wrong in our country … and what we might do to right the capsizing ship of State."
— Peter Coyote, actor and author of *Sleeping Where I Fall*

"Do you care about our democratic freedoms, constitutional government and due process of law? Do you want to pass on these precious gifts to your children and grandchildren? Then read this book — a captivating, lucid account of how our leaders have conspired with private corporations to betray American democracy. Thom Hartmann has given us an excellent guidebook to learn, educate others and organize now, while there's still time."
— David Bollier, author of *Silent Theft: The Private Plunder of Our Common Wealth*

"Finally, the Bush Republicans get the long-form comic history book they deserve."
— Eric Alterman, columnist for *The Nation* and msnbc.com, and author of *What Liberal Media?* and *Who Speaks for America?*

"This is a blockbuster of a book, a thoughtful and highly provocative analysis of American political traditions and our current political situation. An easy and compelling read, it should be on everyone's reading list. You may not agree with all of Hartmann's ideas, but you have to consider them."
— Ken R. Bain, PhD, historian and founding director of the Center for Teaching Excellence at New York University

"Thom Hartmann is a true voice of Wisdom in the bewilderness, and he outlines a clear and inspiring plan to restore government of the people, by the people and for the people, where the government does *the people's* bidding, not the bidding of the highest bidder."
— Steve Bhaerman aka Swami Beyondananda, www.wakeuplaughing.com

"Thom Hartmann's message for everyone (especially the over-stressed and uninformed) should be part of the Western canon. Read this book for a jolt of illumination!"
— Janeane Garofalo, actress (*The Independent* and *Steal This Movie*) and author of *Feel This Book*

"Clear and compelling. Democracy is at risk. Hartmann tells us why. We the People can reclaim democracy. Hartmann tells us how. Read it and act."
— David Korten, co-founder, Positive Futures Network, and author of *When Corporations Rule the World* and *The Post-Corporate World*

"*We the People* is a creative approach to engaging people in an important political debate, and it's sure to be a useful tool for grassroots organizers in the progressive movement."
— John Podesta, President/CEO of Center for American Progress and former Chief of Staff to President Clinton

"This is an excellent tool of popular education. All Americans — young and old — should know what's in this book, especially our youth and those adults lulled to sleep by our entertainment culture. Thank you, Thom Hartmann!"
— Tom Hayden, Former California state assemblyman and senator, and author of *Rebel* and *The Lost Gospel of the Earth*

Reviewers like *We the People* . . .

"*We the People* is a deadly serious comic book that covers virtually all important issues facing Americans and the democracy under which we live. This is one of the most informative and authoritative socio-political analyses of our time. Its warnings and remedies should be taken to heart before the freedoms that we have taken for granted for so long shall be systematically stolen from us.

"You must read this book and urge others to read it."
— Frederick Sweet in *Intervention* magazine

"As a complete work seeking to communicate difficult facts and ideas in a dynamic and accessible way, *We the People* is a fabulous practical manifestation of sequential art's potential. It only feels like a juvenile experience until you realize you just comprehended very mature and profound intricacies in thought and information with less than half the effort one would arguably need to comprehend such things if they were presented in another form."
— Jason Dodd in *BANDOPPLER* magazine

"We were a bit skeptical when his publisher called us about the book, even though we are big Hartmann fans. But once we read a review copy, we were completely won over. This is a great book to read as a sort of one-stop shopping piece on the 'invasion of the democracy snatchers.'

"Actually, we haven't read any other book that covers such sweeping historical, political and corporate collusion issues in such succinct, accessible terms."
— BuzzFlash.com

"This is brilliant! . . . It makes the convoluted ins and outs of politics understandable (our high schooler is gobbling it up right now), and somehow much more personal."
— *Alternatives* Magazine

"Pick up a copy — or ten — and give them to someone you know in junior high school, or a senior citizen, or a busy person who might appreciate an overview with cited sources that takes a surprisingly systemic look at our complex of problems and correspondingly sophisticated set of potential positive paths. The time they take — and the time they save with this entertaining and economical tour de force — may be reflected in the democracy we take back."
— Tom Hastings in *The PeaceWorker*

We the People

★ A CALL TO TAKE BACK AMERICA ★

BY

THOM HARTMANN

ILLUSTRATED BY

NEIL COHN

ADAPTED AND EDITED BY
GENE LATIMER AND PAUL BURKE

CoreWay Media, Inc.
Portland, Oregon

CoreWay Media, Inc., books may be purchased in bulk for educational or grassroots organizing uses, as well as retail sales. Special books or excerpts can also be created to fit
specific needs. For information, please contact:

CoreWay Media, Inc.
3110 SW Arnold Street
Portland OR 97219
www.coreway.com

See www.we-the-people-book.com for further information.

The majority of text has been adapted from a series of essays by Thom Hartmann originally
published on www.commondreams.org.

Publisher's Cataloging-in-Publication
(Provided by Quality Books, Inc.)

Hartmann, Thom, 1951-
    We the People : a call to take back America / Thom
Hartmann ; illustrated by Neil Cohn ; edited and adapted
by Gene Latimer & Paul Burke.
    p. cm.
    Includes bibliographical references and index.
    LCCN 2004101626
    ISBN 1-882109-38-4

    1. United States--Politics and government--2001-
2. Political corruption--United States. 3. Business and
politics--United States. 4. Corporate power--United
States. 5. Political participation--United States.
6. Democracy--United States. I. Cohn, Neil.
II. Latimer, Gene. III. Burke, Paul (Paul W.) IV. Title.

E902.H38 2004   320.973
                       QBI04-200069

ISBN 1-882109-38-4

10 9 8 7 6 5 4 3
Printed in the United States of America on acid-free paper.

Also by Thom Hartmann

*UNEQUAL PROTECTION: The Rise of Corporate Dominance and the Theft of
    Human Rights*
WHAT WOULD JEFFERSON DO? A Return to Democracy
*ULTIMATE SACRIFICE: The Kennedy "Plan for a Coup in Cuba" and the Murder of
J. F. K.*

*THE LAST HOURS OF ANCIENT SUNLIGHT: The Fate of the World and What We
    Can Do Before It's Too Late*
THE PROPHET'S WAY: A Guide to Living in the Now
THE GREATEST SPIRITUAL SECRET OF THE CENTURY

THE EDISON GENE: ADHD and the Gift of the Hunter Child
HEALING ADD: Simple Exercises That Will Change Your Daily Life
ATTENTION DEFICIT DISORDER: A Different Perception
*THOM HARTMANN'S COMPLETE GUIDE TO ADHD: Help for Your Family at Home,
    School and Work*
*ADD SUCCESS STORIES: A Guide to Fulfillment for Families with Attention
    Deficit-Disorder: Maps, Guidebooks, and Travelogues for Hunters in This
    Farmer's World*
BEYOND ADD: Hunting for Reasons in the Past & Present
*ADHD SECRETS OF SUCCESS: Coaching Yourself to Fulfillment in the Business
    World*
THINK FAST! The ADD Experience

Also by Neil Cohn

EARLY WRITINGS ON VISUAL LANGUAGE
MEDITATIONS: 1998 - 2002

★★★★ TABLE OF CONTENTS ★★★★

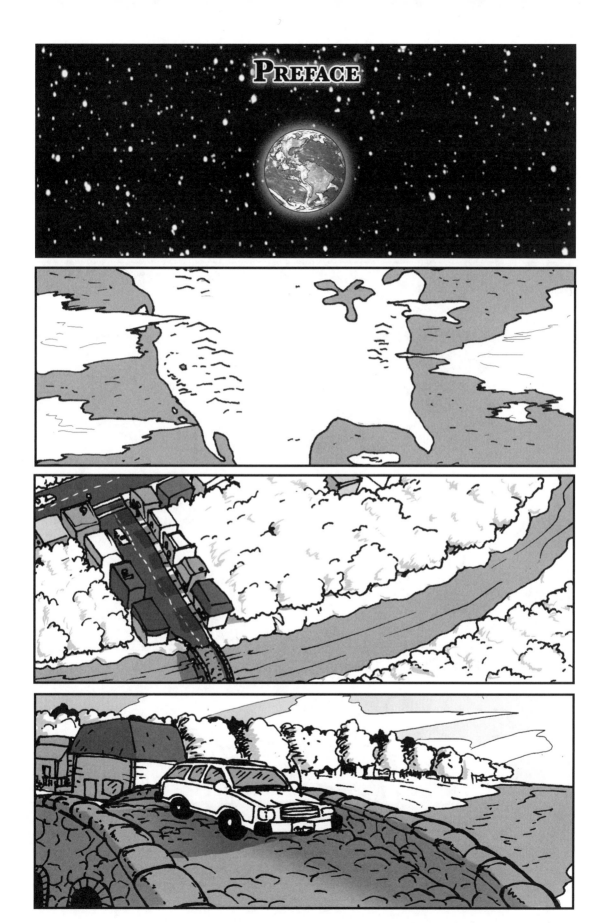

THE EMPIRE'S NEW CLOTHES

Sigh

AMERICA AT WAR

ATTACKED IN THE NORTHERN PAR

"The news from the war is not good today..."

Is this war business about something even more insidious than oil?

Isn't it really about the end of democracy itself...

Can you please remove your shoes, sir?

...carefully planned by a small group of cynical intellectuals who truly believe that democracy is cute and quaint but that only an all-powerful government can guarantee stability in a dangerous world?

4

A DISTURBING SCENARIO...

The nation's leader knew that there were plans for a major act of terrorism against the country.

Previous attempts had failed, but he knew it was only a matter of time before they'd succeed.

Finally, in a bold terrorist act, a major national symbol was destroyed, and the leader used the opportunity to declare a "war on terrorism"…

…and establish his legitimacy as a leader — even though he hadn't won a majority in the previous election.

He referred to the heinous act as "a sign from God" and declared an all-out war on terrorism and its ideological sponsors:

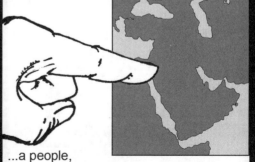

…a people, he said, who traced their origins to the Middle East and found motivation for their "evil" deeds in their religion.

Soon, the first prison was holding terrorism suspects.

In a national outburst of patriotism, flags were displayed everywhere, even printed in newspapers.

Within weeks of the terrorist attack — in the name of combating terrorism and fighting the philosophy he said spawned it — the nation's now-popular leader pushed through legislation that suspended constitutional guarantees of

- free speech,
- privacy, and
- habeas corpus.

Police could now intercept mail...

...and wiretap phones.

Suspected terrorists could be imprisoned without specific charges and without access to their lawyers.

Police could sneak into people's homes without warrants if the cases involved terrorism.

To get his patriotic act passed over the objections of concerned legislators and civil libertarians, he agreed to put a "sunset" (expiration) provision on it.

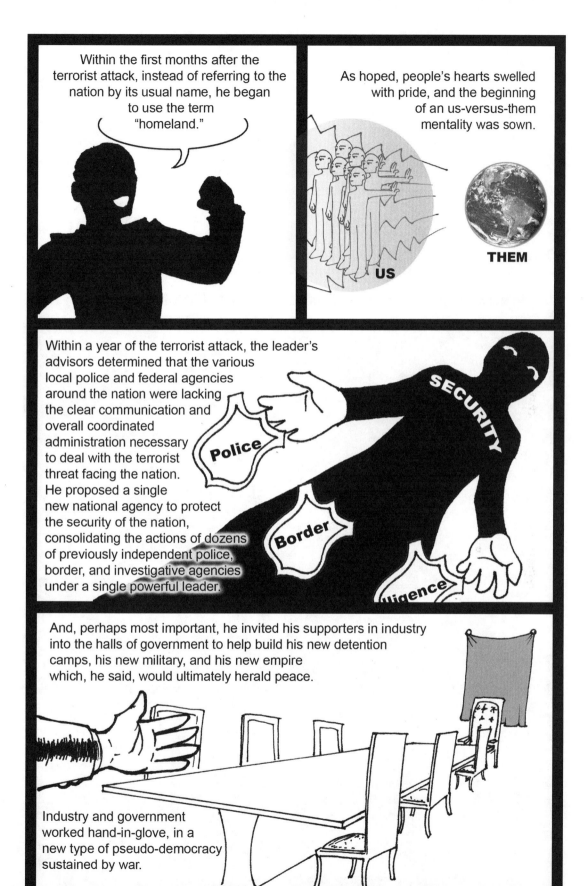

Within the first months after the terrorist attack, instead of referring to the nation by its usual name, he began to use the term "homeland."

As hoped, people's hearts swelled with pride, and the beginning of an us-versus-them mentality was sown.

US

THEM

Within a year of the terrorist attack, the leader's advisors determined that the various local police and federal agencies around the nation were lacking the clear communication and overall coordinated administration necessary to deal with the terrorist threat facing the nation. He proposed a single new national agency to protect the security of the nation, consolidating the actions of dozens of previously independent police, border, and investigative agencies under a single powerful leader.

SECURITY

Police

Border

lligence

And, perhaps most important, he invited his supporters in industry into the halls of government to help build his new detention camps, his new military, and his new empire which, he said, would ultimately herald peace.

Industry and government worked hand-in-glove, in a new type of pseudo-democracy sustained by war.

I don't know what that brings up for you, but...

...this scenario is actually 70 years old.

The time is 1933. The leader is Hitler.

The Reichstag — Germany's parliament building — was gutted by a fire started by a Dutch terrorist.

HOMELAND

HEIMAT*

Americans remember Hitler's Office of Reich Security (the Reichssicherheitshauptamt) simply by its most famous agency's (the Schutzstaffel) initials:

the S.S.

And you know the rest of the story.

*"Heimat" translates as "homeland."

8

OUR ORWELLIAN REALITY

War is Peace

BIG BROTHER IS WATCHING YOU

George Orwell's novel, *1984*, paints a chilling portrait of government control that is becoming all too recognizable in America today.

1984
George Orwell

For instance, the way Orwell's seemingly democratic president kept his nation in a constant state of repression was by having a perpetual war.

Cynics suggest the lesson wasn't lost on Lyndon Johnson or Richard Nixon...

VIETNAM

...who both, they say, extended the Vietnam War so it coincidentally ran over election cycles...

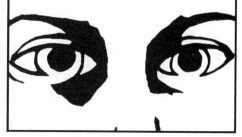

...knowing that a wartime president is more likely to be re-elected and has more power than a president in peacetime.

WAR IS THE ENEMY

Orwell's idea that perpetual war was a masterful technique for repressing the masses wasn't new, however.

On April 20, 1795, James Madison, who helped shepherd through the Constitution and Bill of Rights and would become president of the United States in the following decade, wrote:

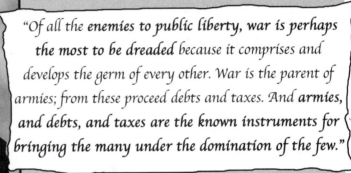

"Of all the enemies to public liberty, war is perhaps the most to be dreaded because it comprises and develops the germ of every other. War is the parent of armies; from these proceed debts and taxes. And armies, and debts, and taxes are the known instruments for bringing the many under the domination of the few."

Reflecting on war's impact on the presidency, Madison continued his letter about the dangerous and intoxicating power of war.

"In war, too, the discretionary power of the Executive [Presidency] is extended... Its influence in dealing out offices, honors, and emoluments [profits] is multiplied; and all the means of seducing the minds, are added to those of subduing the force of the people. The same malignant aspect in republicanism may be traced in the inequality of fortunes, and the opportunities of fraud, growing out of a state of war... and in the degeneracy of manners and morals, engendered by both.

"No nation..."

-he concluded-

..."could preserve its freedom in the midst of continual warfare."

Once the Revolutionary War was over, and the Constitution had been worked out and presented to the states for ratification...

Thomas Jefferson turned his attention to what he and Madison felt was a terrible inadequacy in the new Constitution: it didn't explicitly stipulate the "natural rights" of the new nation's citizens...

...and didn't protect against the rise of new commercial monopolies like the East India Company–

–which had once dominated life in the colonies and used the British army as its own private army.

On December 20th, 1787, Jefferson wrote to James Madison about his concerns regarding the Constitution. He said, bluntly, that it was deficient in several areas.

"I will now tell you what I do not like...First, the omission of a bill of rights, providing clearly, and without the aid of sophism, for freedom of religion, freedom of the press, protection against standing armies, restriction of commercial monopolies, the eternal and unremitting force of the habeas corpus laws, and trials by jury in all matters of fact triable by the laws of the land, and not by the laws of nations."

When the United States was first declared independent in 1776, its Founders knew humans had previously faced tyranny in the form of despotic kings and inquisitional churches.

The Bill of Rights firmly declared that no church could ever again control a democratic government.

Bill of Rights
Congress of the United States.

And the Declaration of Independence made it clear right from the beginning that, when citizens are burdened by "a design to reduce them under absolute Despotism, it is their right, it is their duty, to throw off such Government..."

11

Thus, the Founders and the Framers disposed of despotism by church or state, guaranteeing the absolute and inviolable rights of a nation's citizens to life, liberty, and the pursuit of happiness.

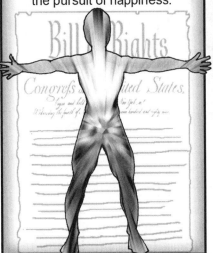

But there was a third entity that Thomas Jefferson and others worried may also one day rise to seize control of the government and enslave the people.

James Madison wrote...

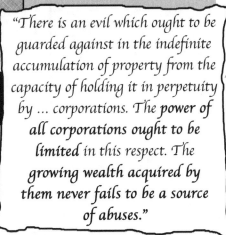

*"There is an evil which ought to be guarded against in the indefinite accumulation of property from the capacity of holding it in perpetuity by ... corporations. The **power of all corporations ought to be limited** in this respect. The **growing wealth acquired by them never fails to be a source of abuses.**"*

In 1787 Jefferson proposed an additional amendment to the Bill of Rights to restrain corporations, calling for a constitutional amendment to "ban monopolies in commerce," although it failed under the Federalist opposition of the Hamilton/Adams faction.

In arguing for a ban on commercial monopolies, the Founders, who had just fought a war of independence against both Britain and the world's largest transnational corporation (The East India Company, whose tea they'd thrown into Boston Harbor), knew the danger of corporations becoming so powerful they could influence government the way the East India Company had persuaded England for the tax reduction and free trade agreement that came to be known as the Tea Act of 1773.

But it's not just Madison and Jefferson's remarkable foresight that's warning us. More recent presidents have also noted the danger of a corporate usurpation of democracy, particularly when fed by the bloody meat of war.

As he was leaving office in 1961, President Dwight D. Eisenhower had looked back over his years as president, as a general and as supreme commander of the Allied Forces in France during World War II, and noted that the Cold War had brought a new, Orwellian type of war to the American landscape — a perpetual war supported by a perpetual war industry.

It was the confluence of the two things Jefferson had warned against, and had tried to ban in his first proposed version of the Bill of Rights.

In a nationally-televised speech, Eisenhower spoke in sobering tones of how the United States had never had an armaments industry until World War II and the Korean War.

But, the world situation had compelled it to...

"create a permanent armaments industry of vast proportions."

At the same time, the defense establishment was dramatically expanding. In that context, he delivered the following warning:

"**This conjunction of an immense military establishment and a large arms industry is new in the American experience. The total influence, economic, political, even spiritual, is felt in every city, every Statehouse, every office of the Federal government.** We recognize the imperative need for this development. Yet **we must not fail to comprehend its grave implications.** Our toil, resources and livelihood are all involved; so is the very structure of our society.

"In the councils of government, we must guard against the acquisition of unwarranted influence, whether sought or unsought, by the military-industrial complex. The potential for the disastrous rise of misplaced power exists and will persist.

He concluded with a very specific warning to us, the generation that would follow...

"We must never let the weight of this combination endanger our liberties or democratic processes. ... We should take nothing for granted. Only an **alert and knowledgeable citizenry** can compel the proper meshing of the huge industrial and military machinery of defense with our peaceful methods and goals, so that **security and liberty may prosper together.**"

War, Profit and Human Values

In the late 20th and early 21st centuries, Madison's and Eisenhower's warnings become more of a concern.

War has become big business in America...

...and we're now not only a big user of military equipment, we sell it to the world. We're the world's largest exporter of weapons of virtually all sizes and types.

UNCLE SAM'S ARMS SALE

But military spending is the least effective way to stimulate or sustain an economy for a very simple reason:

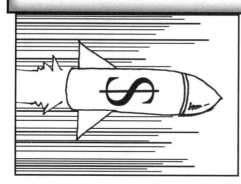

...military products are used once and destroyed.

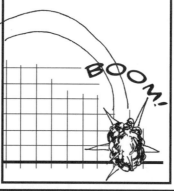

When a government uses taxpayer money to build a bridge or highway or hospital, that investment will be used for decades, perhaps centuries, and will continue to fuel economic activity throughout its lifetime.

But when taxpayer dollars are used to build a bomb or a bullet, that military hardware will be used once and then vanish. As it vanishes, so does the wealth it represented...

...never to be recovered.

Today, as we face international financial and domestic political crises, it's useful to remember that the ravages of the Great Depression hit Germany and the United States alike.

Through the 1930s, however, Roosevelt and Hitler chose very different courses to bring their nations back to power and prosperity.

Germany's response was to merge corporations into government (creating unequal protection for working citizens), to privatize much of what was held in ownership for the people and administered by the government (i.e., "the Commons")...

...and to create an illusion of prosperity through continual and ever-expanding war.

America, on the other hand, passed minimum wage laws to raise the middle class, increased taxes on corporations and the wealthiest individuals, created Social Security, and became the employer of last resort through public works programs like the WPA.

As Eisenhower said in an April, 1953 speech:

"Every gun that is made, every warship launched, every rocket fired, signifies, in the final sense, a theft from those who hunger and are not fed, those who are cold and are not clothed. The world in arms is not spending money alone. It is spending the **sweat of its laborers, the genius of its scientists, the hopes of its children.**"

It was a brilliant articulation of human needs in a world increasingly dominated by the non-breathing entities called corporations whose values are profit and growth...

...but not the human values of fresh air, clean water, pure food, freedom, and happiness.

But it was a call unheeded and, today, it is nearly totally forgotten.

Now, our nation has a corporate support group anxious to help a war-intoxicated president rationalize the diversion of taxpayer dollars toward military uses and away from "soft" causes like "quality of life" here at home, or alternative forms of energy to make us less dependent on foreign oil-producing states.

THE TAKEOVER IS NEARLY COMPLETE

During the Great Depression, President Franklin Delano Roosevelt once said..

"There is a mysterious cycle in human events. To some generations much is given. Of other generations much is expected. **This generation of Americans has a rendezvous with destiny."**

At the beginning of the 21st century, it seems that history does repeat itself.

Today, James Madison's warning about an Executive Branch beholden to "commercial monopolies" and intoxicated by war takes on a new and vivid meaning.

And to the extent that our Constitution is still intact, the choice is again ours as to which path we'll pursue.

The takeover of our democracy is nearly complete.

A third world war would not only vastly enrich the transnationals who have perpetrated this coup...

...but could also mean the end of the first experiment with republican democracy in almost three thousand years.

War is like the magic trick in *The Wizard of Oz*...

WIZARD

ILLUSION

...it hides the failures and crimes of political leaders and their friends. But behind them lies the real power—

"the men behind the screen."

POLITICIANS

$

And they're not men at all — they're non-living, non-breathing legal fictions which have claimed the rights of humans to seize control of democracies from one side of the Atlantic to the other.

My fellow citizens, I'm afraid that this country is facing a new version of feudalism, the kind of corporate feudalism that Italian dictator Benito Mussolini called fascism.

Are you serious? "Fascism" in America?

Yes, I'm quite serious. Let me lay some historical foundation for you.

The Founders of America knew that for 6,000 years "civilized" humans had always been ruled by one of three types of leaders:

1776

1. Kings

Kings ruled the population by virtue of the power of their armies, the threat of continual warfare, and the willingness to use violence and terror. The first of such rulers were warlords like Gilgamesh. We find the remnants of their rule in the dungeons of British castles and the palaces of Middle Eastern kingdoms.

2. Theocrats

Theocrats and popes held power because of the people's fear of a god or gods. They claimed that their particular god had given them the right to rule.

We hear the remnants of their rule echoing in Osama bin Laden's still-fresh anger over the Crusades and a right-wing Christian leader's claim that 9-11 was his god's way of punishing America for not listening to him.

3. Feudal Lords

Feudal lords held the society's greatest wealth, owned the apparatus of governance and had absolute control over the lives of most people, including the power to throw average people into poverty. Aristocrats and plutocrats ruled by using the Calvinist and neo-Darwinist claim that great wealth was a sign from the gods or nature of a moral worthiness and destiny to rule. We find evidence of modern feudalism in the fact that former Enron executive and number one contributor to the George W. Bush campaign, Ken Lay, once had a desk in the Bush White House.

19

Then came the Athenian Greeks, with their 200+ year experiment in democracy...

...and, two millennia later, Jefferson, Adams, Franklin, and the other Founders, with the idea of trying it again.

The "new" idea of our Founders in 1776 was to throw off all three of these historic tyrannies and replace them with a fourth way:

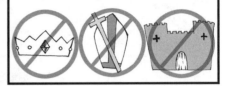

People being ruled by themselves.

It was the noble experiment of creating a government whose leaders drew their power, their legitimacy, and their authority solely from the consent of the governed...

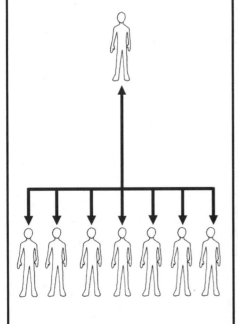

...rule by

We the People

They called it a...

Republican Democracy.

Tested by other nations, by civil war, and by economic disasters, it seemed at once fragile and powerful.

It was an experiment that, while young and unproven on the grand stage of civilization, just might succeed in outlasting that of its Greek progenitors.

The basis of its strength was "the consent of the people."

So, America's Founders and Framers identified, declared war against, and fought and died to keep the three historic forms of tyranny —

Kingdom

Theocracy

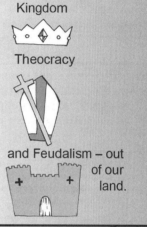

and Feudalism – out of our land.

Kings would never again be allowed to govern America, the Founders said...

OW!

And don't come back!

...so they stripped the president of the power to declare war.

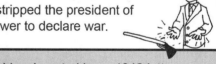

As Lincoln noted in an 1848 letter:

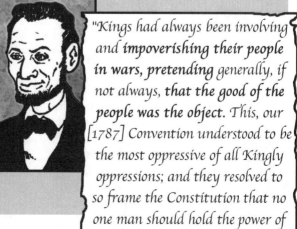

"Kings had always been involving and **impoverishing their people in wars, pretending** generally, if not always, **that the good of the people was the object.** This, our [1787] Convention understood to be the most oppressive of all Kingly oppressions; and they resolved to so frame the Constitution that no one man should hold the power of bringing this oppression upon us."

Theocrats would never again be allowed to govern America, as they had tried in the early Puritan communities.

OW!

And stay out!

In 1784, when Patrick Henry proposed that the Virginia legislature use a sort of faith-based voucher system to pay for "Christian education," James Madison responded with ferocity, saying government support of church teachings

"will be a dangerous abuse of power."

He added...

"The Rulers who are guilty of such an encroachment exceed the commission from which they derive their authority, and are Tyrants. The People who submit to it are governed by laws made neither by themselves nor by an authority derived from them, and are slaves."

And America was not conceived of as a feudal state, feudalism being broadly defined as "rule by the super-rich."

OW! I'll be back!

Yah, yah... Out!

Rather, our nation was created in large part in reaction to centuries of European feudalism.

In his December 1, 1863, lecture, "The Fortune of the Republic," Ralph Waldo Emerson said,

"We began with freedom. America was opened after the feudal mischief was spent. No inquisitions here, no kings, no nobles, no dominant church."

The great and revolutionary ideal of America is that a government can exist while drawing its authority, power, and ongoing legitimacy from a single source:

"The consent of the governed."

Once again, however, conservatives would like to change all that.

Which is why we, as citizens of America, now have our own "rendevous with destiny."

What the conservatives are really arguing for is a return to a historic form of tyranny.

Back in 1983, before its publisher (Houghton Mifflin Company) was acquired by a multinational corporation, the American Heritage Dictionary left us this definition of the form of government the democracies of Spain, Italy, and Germany had morphed into during the 1930s:

"fas-cism (fâsh'iz'em) n. A system of government that exercises a dictatorship of the extreme right, typically through the merging of state and business leadership, together with belligerent nationalism."

The key to fascism is the merging of state and corporate interests.

It is "corporatism," to use Mussolini's word, which he later renamed "fascism."

It's simply the modern version of feudalism.

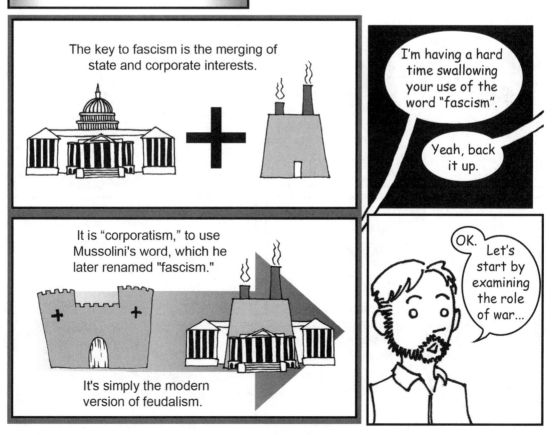

Americans and foreign observers have struggled to explain and understand the Bush administration's invasion of Iraq.

THE USES OF WAR

And the administration has tried out a whole series of explanations to justify their actions...

Democracy

9-11

Middle East stability

Iraqi liberation

Harboring terrorists

Weapons of mass destruction

Where do you weigh in on this, Thom?

ON AIR

Well, I tell you...

...all of the president's explanations fell away as I was pumping gas one day at the airport and spilled some of it on my hand.

I immediately thought of it as "dinosaur blood," and I realized that Bush's war was never about anything else.

Of course, the gasoline that refills my rental cars and the refined kerosene that fuels the planes I fly in aren't really dinosaur blood; they're far more ancient than any tyrannosaurus, brontosaurus or similar bones ever found.

MOM?

SNIFF

Those guys vanished around 65 million years ago.

HEY, YOU SMELL SOMETHING?

But the fossilized plants and bacteria that actually made my gasoline are 300 to 400 million years old. By the time dinosaurs ruled the Earth, pretty much all of the planet's oil was already created.

Strange, when you consider it in those terms, that we'd base a nation's foreign policy on a limited supply of fossils older than the dinosaurs.

National Energy Policy

But, we do. So, in order to understand the war strategies or any of the other hidden agendas of this administration, we have to follow the money and we have to follow the oil.

What do you mean by "follow the oil?"

Well, American automobile manufacturers must meet or exceed minimum federal fuel economy goals ("fleet mileage standards") for their total automobile production.

SUVs are treated like trucks, which are not subject to the auto standards.

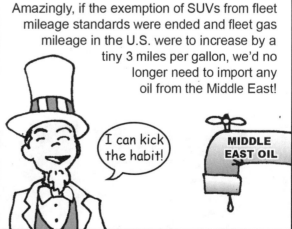
Amazingly, if the exemption of SUVs from fleet mileage standards were ended and fleet gas mileage in the U.S. were to increase by a tiny 3 miles per gallon, we'd no longer need to import any oil from the Middle East!

I can kick the habit!

MIDDLE EAST OIL

But the larger the car, the larger the profit for both the oil and the auto companies, and the auto and oil lobbies pass out millions of dollars to our congresspeople and senators in Washington, DC.

And now that the airwaves have been sold to corporate interests who will allow politicians to speak only if they pay, political campaigns guzzle cash like SUVs guzzle gas.

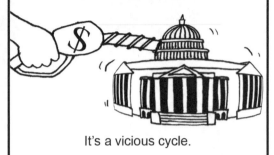

It's a vicious cycle.

Just consider what we could accomplish if we were to institute an accelerated energy-independence program along the lines of the Manhattan Project, which built the first atomic bomb...

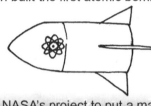

...or NASA's project to put a man on the moon?

Such a visionary program could lead to a major boost in small-scale, local generation of electricity (about a tenth of all electricity generated in the US is lost through transmission over long high-tension lines, and steam generating plants only convert about a third of their heat energy to electricity, wasting the other two-thirds). In addition, with the development of hydrogen energy technologies, we could free states from the tyranny of out-of-state energy companies manipulating their supplies and prices, and clean up our air as well.

Not only that, but decentralized power generation could help us overcome the structural weaknesses in systems like the brittle electric grid that plunged the eastern heart of North America into darkness in the summer of 2003.

Then, if we were to encourage Victory Garden types of local agriculture and homestead farming, making it again patriotic to replace back yards of grass with vegetables (as it was during WWII)...

...we could eliminate our absolute dependence on factory farming systems that now require billions of gallons of oil for production and transportation...

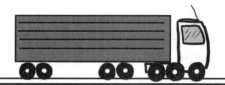

...that deliver foods laden with oil-derived pesticides, herbicides, and preservatives to our tables, and that render our irreplaceable topsoil sterile.

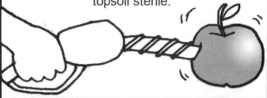

Most important, we would no longer feel forced to permanently occupy the world's oil-producing regions.

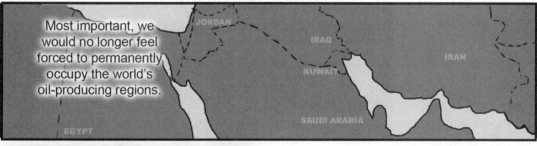

But a government whose policies have been captured by:

big oil

big auto

...and big agriculture –

– a few dozen corporations that are each richer than the majority of nations on earth –

– refuses to consider such rational alternatives to our continued dependence on imported oil.

Are you saying that the Administration doesn't care that we're energy-dependent?

Well, a few years ago, the first President Bush frankly admitted that America is only a small portion of the world's population, yet uses a large percentage of the world's oil and other natural resources...

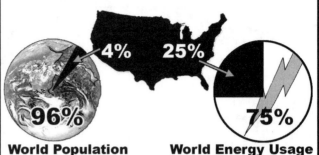

4% **25%**

96% **75%**

World Population **World Energy Usage**

"The American lifestyle is not negotiable."

America has no plans to kick its addictions to...

...McMansions for two-person families...

...a transportation infrastructure based on 6,000-pound SUVs carrying single individuals...

...cheap Chinese goods at Wal-Mart and cheap Mexican produce in the supermarket...

We're king of the hill, and we intend to stay that way, even if it means going to war to keep it.

The Bush administration has a clear and specific vision for the future of America and the world, and they believe it's a positive one.

In order to put forward an alternative vision, it's essential to first understand that, at its core, the dream for America held by the New Right is authoritarian, elitist/aristocratic, and grounded in belligerent nationalism.

SNAP!

It's strikingly similar to the world-view held by imperial Rome, and by Mussolini, Hitler, and Generalissimo Franco of Spain, a vision that says that if we're not the most powerful in the world, we'll always be at risk.

It's a vision driven by fear, and grounded in a psychological inability to trust others.

The arrogant imperialist aspects of this vision were first publicly articulated on June 3, 1997, in the Statement of Principles put forth by the

Project for the New American Century.

Signed by now Vice President Dick Cheney, now Secretary of Defense Donald Rumsfeld, now Undersecretary of Defense Paul Wolfowitz, professional moralist Bill Bennett, Florida Governor Jeb Bush, political activist Gary Bauer, the National Security Council's Elliott Abrams, and publisher and former presidential candidate Steve Forbes and others from the Reagan/Bush administration...

...it clearly stated that "the history of this century should have taught us to embrace the cause of American leadership."

Can you give me an example of how that plays out in the world?

Yeah, let's look at how such "American leadership" has led us into the quagmires of Vietnam, Afghanistan, and Iraq.

29

When the administration's people say American involvement in Iraq, for example, is:

"not about oil,"

...they're often responding to charges that they're only going after profits for American oil companies.

They speak truth, in that context, when they say the war isn't about revenues from oil — the profits will only be a desirable side effect.

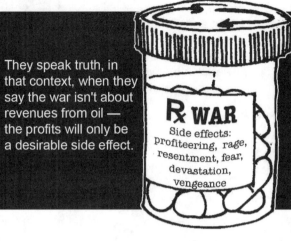

Rx WAR

Side effects: profiteering, rage, resentment, fear, devastation, vengeance

---

What the war is really about is the survival of the American lifestyle...

...which, in their world-view, is both non-negotiable...

...and based almost entirely on access to cheap oil.

The same year Cheney and the others wrote their papers on The New American Century, I wrote a book about the coming end of American peace and prosperity because of our dependence on a dwindling supply of oil.

"Since the discovery of oil in Titusville, PA, where the world's first oil well was drilled in 1859"...

...I wrote in *The Last Hours of Ancient Sunlight*...

..."humans have extracted 742 billion barrels of oil from the Earth. Currently, world oil reserves are estimated at about 1,000 billion barrels, which will last (according to the most optimistic estimates of the oil industry) for almost 45 years at current rates of consumption."

But that doesn't mean that we'll suck on the straw for 45 years and then it'll suddenly stop.

When about half the oil has been removed from an underground oil field, it starts to get much harder (and thus more expensive) to extract the remaining half.

The last third to quarter can be excruciatingly expensive to extract — so much so that wells these days that have hit that point are usually just capped because it costs more to extract the oil than it can be sold for, or it's more profitable to ship oil in from the Middle East, even after accounting for the cost of shipping.

The halfway point in the lifetime of an oil field is referred to as "The Hubbert Peak," after scientist M. King Hubbert, who first pointed this out in 1956 and projected 1970 as the year for the Hubbert Peak of US oil supplies.

Hubbert was off by four years — 1974 saw the initial decline in US oil production and the consequent rise in price.

In 1975, Hubbert, who is now deceased, projected that we would see a world-wide Hubbert Peak in the year 2000. Once that point had been hit, he and other experts suggested, the world could expect economy-destabilizing spikes in the price of oil, and wars over control of this vital resource.

Most of the world has now been digitally "X-rayed," using satellites, seismic data, and computers, in the process of locating 41,000 oil fields.

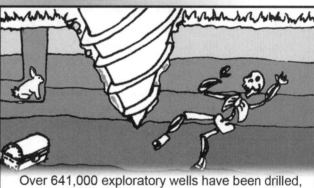

Over 641,000 exploratory wells have been drilled, and virtually all fields that show any promise are factored into the one trillion barrel estimate the oil industry uses for world oil reserves.

Of those 1 trillion barrels, Saudi Arabia has about 259 billion barrels.

Iraq is estimated by the U.S. government to have 432 billion barrels, although at the moment only about 112 billion barrels have been tapped.

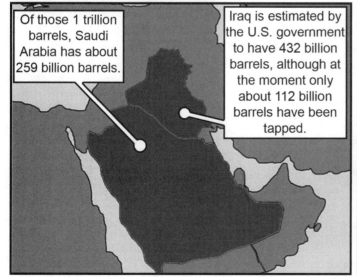

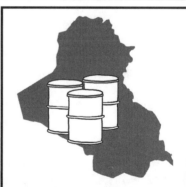

The rest — virgin oil — can be pumped out for as little as $1.50 a barrel, making Iraqi oil not only among the most abundant in the world...

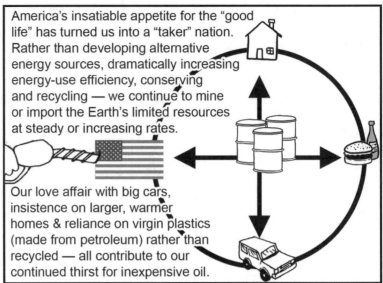

America's insatiable appetite for the "good life" has turned us into a "taker" nation. Rather than developing alternative energy sources, dramatically increasing energy-use efficiency, conserving and recycling — we continue to mine or import the Earth's limited resources at steady or increasing rates.

Our love affair with big cars, insistence on larger, warmer homes & reliance on virgin plastics (made from petroleum) rather than recycled — all contribute to our continued thirst for inexpensive oil.

...but the most profitable, at a time when virtually all American oil fields (except the Alaska North Slope) have dwindled past the Hubbert Peak into $5 to $25 per barrel pumping costs.

If we assume that the American people won't tolerate a change in this lifestyle...

...then we can conclude that our very security as a stable democracy is dependent on a cheap oil supply.

And it seems that the backroom architects of the New American Century — men like Cheney, Wolfowitz and cohort Richard Pearle — drew a bead on where they'd get the oil to guarantee the viability of this American "way of life" a long time ago.

Documents pried loose in a Judicial Watch lawsuit regarding the secret meetings of Cheney's National Energy Policy task force* show that the vice president and his buddies from Enron and other energy companies had already drawn up maps of Iraq's oil fields ...

* (http://www.judicialwatch.org/071703.c_.shtml)

...and made lists of potential corporate purchasers of Iraqi oil months before the horrific events of 9/11/01 and the declaration of the "war on terror."

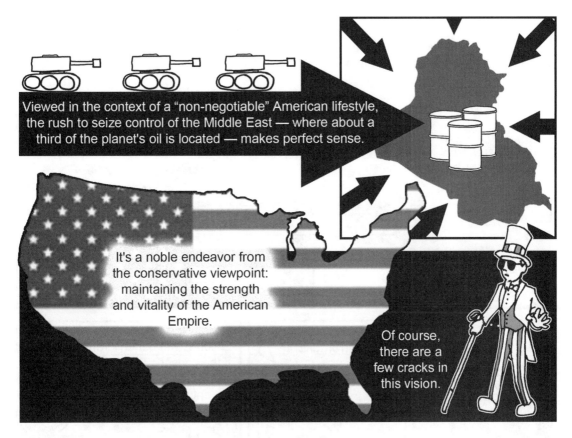

Viewed in the context of a "non-negotiable" American lifestyle, the rush to seize control of the Middle East — where about a third of the planet's oil is located — makes perfect sense.

It's a noble endeavor from the conservative viewpoint: maintaining the strength and vitality of the American Empire.

Of course, there are a few cracks in this vision.

In order to have such a New American Century...

...we must be willing to foul our waters and air with the byproducts of oil combustion and oil-fired power plants...

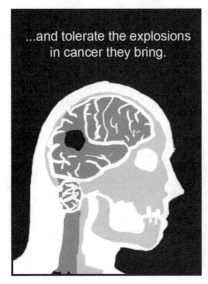

...and tolerate the explosions in cancer they bring.

We must be willing to gamble that raising CO_2 levels won't destabilize the atmosphere and tip us into a new Ice Age by shutting down the Great Conveyor Belt warm-water currents in the Atlantic.

Welcome to FLORIDA!

We must be willing to hold the rest of the world off at the point of a bayonet...

Don't be a bully.

...and to take on the England/Northern Ireland and Israel/Palestine type of terrorism that inevitably comes when people decide to assert nationalism and confront empire.

That, my friend, means perpetual war.

Perpetual war?

Yes, unfortunately...

...that's the prognosis for us, our children and our children's children if the conservatives' vision is allowed to continue driving America's actions.

Sigh

ON AIR

34

But, perhaps most distressing...

...the third George to be President of the United States must be willing to clamp down on his own dissident citizens the same way that King George III of England did in 1776.

These are the requirements of empire.

The last American statesman to put forth a different vision was President Jimmy Carter, who candidly pointed out in the late seventies that oil was a dwindling domestic resource.

Carter said that we mustn't find ourselves in a position of having to fight wars to seize other people's oil...

...and that a decade or two of transition to renewable energy sources would ensure the stability and future of America without destabilizing the rest of the world.

About time!

MIDDLE EAST OIL

It would even lead to a cleaner environment and a better quality of life.

Carter put in place energy tax credits and incentives that birthed an exploding new industry based on building...

...solar-heated homes...

...windmill-powered communities...

...and the development of alternatives to petroleum fuels.

But one of the first official acts of office of the next president, Ronald Reagan, was to remove Carter's solar panels from the roof of the White House in 1981.

He then repealed Carter's tax incentives for renewable energy and killed off an entire industry.

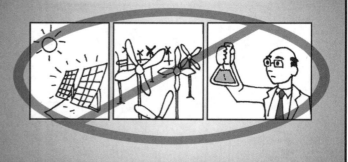

No president since then has had the courage or vision to face the hard reality that Carter shared with us.

And now you can see the irony.

Osama bin Laden, for example, explicitly said that he attacked the U.S. because we had troops stationed on the holy soil of his homeland —

Go home!

— a position not that different from Northern Irish, Palestinian, Tamil, and Kashmiri terrorists.

And our troops were put there to protect our access to Saudi oil, a legacy of dependence we inherited from Reagan after his rejection of Carter's initiatives.

But how different is this, really, from what other industrialized countries are doing?

Good question. I visited Germany not too long ago...

My friend Samuel picked me up from the train station.

Your car's exhaust smells like French fries.

36

It's because it's running on oil, possibly recycled from a restaurant. It's a diesel engine modified to run on vegetable oil.

Interestingly, here in Germany you can buy "bio-diesel" or recycled vegetable oil at gas stations...

...while in England people who modify their diesel cars to run on vegetable oil are vilified and even prosecuted.

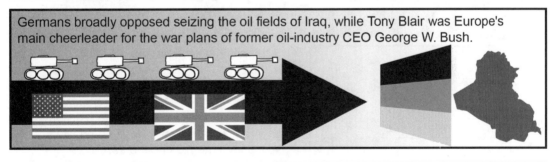

Germans broadly opposed seizing the oil fields of Iraq, while Tony Blair was Europe's main cheerleader for the war plans of former oil-industry CEO George W. Bush.

Germany is not an oil-producing nation, and the typical German consumes less than half the overall energy and oil of the typical American.

The German government offers incentives to architects and companies to design and build energy-efficient or even energy-producing (as in active or passive solar, etc.) buildings...

...and public transportation (particularly the train system) is cheap, efficient, and very well maintained.

England is an oil-producing nation, and the oil lobby in the UK, like in the U.S., is powerful.

At the same time, securing the oil of the Middle East, perhaps with England's biggest oil companies as partners in the pumping consortium that will undoubtedly come out of an Iraqi war effort, was promoted to the British public by the corporate-owned British newspapers and similarly corporate-loyal UK politicians.

In England using French-fry oil to power your car is considered unpatriotic, and can even land you in court.

Meanwhile, the British rail system is a mess...

...and their highways are hopelessly clogged with cars, cars, and more cars.

All running on fossil oil.

It's not surprising to me that a country like Germany, that remembers well the blood cost of war, is quickly moving toward energy efficiency and oil-independence, has no domestic Big Oil lobby pushing its newspapers and politicians, and would oppose its own children dying in a faraway war to secure a vast oil supply.

After all, they've figured out what to do with all that the grease that the fast-food joints once poured down the drain. And, since burning vegetable oil is cheaper, less polluting, and doesn't require a distant army to maintain, they seem to be having a good time making the transition.

The car smells nice, eh? Builds your appetite for dinner!

HA! HA!

THE "WAR ON TERRORISM"

How does the war on terrorism fit in with all of this?

Let's look at some of our recent history on that front.

Timothy McVeigh's inspiration for the 1996 bombing of the Murrah Federal Building in Oklahoma City came from William Pierce's apocalyptic novel:

THE TURNER DIARIES

...which ends with a worldwide Armageddon-style holocaust in which only white Anglo-Saxon Protestants are left standing.

In the book, the U.S. government responds to a terrorist attack (the bombing of a federal building in Oklahoma) by cracking down on dissent...

...expanding the power of the Executive Branch...

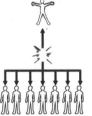

...and shredding constitutional civil rights protections.

Bill of Rights
Congress of the United States

White "patriots" respond by declaring war against the government that had once tried to take away their guns.

Thus begins the cycle of violence that ends with the ultimate worldwide war, a vision straight out of the Book of Revelation.

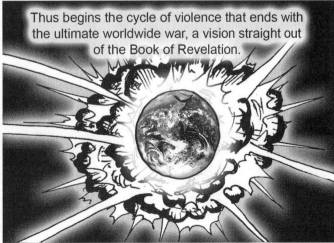

But McVeigh's expectation of a repressive federal reaction to his right-wing terrorism ran into a snag.

Bill Clinton knew the difference between a rogue nation and a rogue criminal.

Like every President since George Washington, Clinton knew that nations declare war only against other nations.

NATION   NATION

While armies deal with rogue states, police deal with criminals, be they domestic or international.

Like Germany's response to the Red Army Faction, Italy's response to The Red Brigades, and Greece's response to the "17 November" group (among others)*, Clinton brought the full force of the criminal justice system against McVeigh, and even had Interpol and overseas police agencies looking for possible McVeigh accomplices.

The result was that the trauma of the Oklahoma City terrorist bombing was limited...

...closure was achieved for its victims...

...the civil rights of Americans were largely left intact...

Bill of Rights
Congress of the United States.

...and the United States government was able to get back to its constitutionally-defined job of ensuring life, liberty, and the pursuit of happiness for its citizens.

* European terrorist organizations that arose from the late 1960s on.

Although numerous recent presidents have declared "wars" on abstractions like

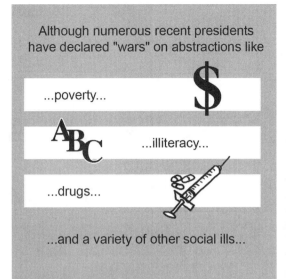

...poverty...

...illiteracy...

...drugs...

...and a variety of other social ills...

...all were well aware that these so-called "wars" were, in truth, just politically useful rhetoric.

Real war can only be declared by one nation against another...

NATION   NATION

It's not possible to declare a war against an abstraction.

The crime of 9-11 has been often cited to rationalize the loss of civil liberties and the continued traumatizing of the American people with regular "Terror Alerts" and a never-ending "war on terror."

But 9-11 wasn't an act of war, because it wasn't done against us by a nation.

It was, instead, a crime, perpetrated by a criminal and his followers.

NATION

It was a horrific crime, certainly.

A crime that required strong, swift, and sure response. A crime that other nations, corporations, and individuals may have abetted and must be held accountable for both domestically and in the international venues of the United Nations and the International Criminal Court.

A crime deserving a thorough investigation (which the Bush administration stonewalled for 2 1/2 years and which has yet to provide results).

Meanwhile, Osama bin Laden and al Qaeda are not nations. Bin Laden was a criminal, and his group was a Middle Eastern sort of mafia with terrorist ambitions, initially funded by his father...

...who was coincidentally a business partner with George W. Bush's father (our 41st president).

To continue using our military against a criminal organization only compounds the horrific crime of 9-11, because armies aren't particularly good at police work.

It's time to restore civil liberties to Americans...

...rein in an Executive Branch intoxicated by warfare...

...hand over to American and international police agencies the very real and very big job of dealing with the remnants of al Qaeda around the world...

Anything less simply perpetuates the crimes.

For as James Madison once warned us...

...and prevent a recurrence of 9-11 by *fully* investigating who was involved and how they pulled it off in the first place.

"No nation could preserve its freedom in the midst of continual warfare."

DROWNING DEMOCRACY

As the scenario from 1933 Germany reminds us, war is a time-tested and proven way of diverting a citizenry's attention away from domestic problems or a leader's past.

Many — particularly political and editorial voices in Europe — have suggested that the Bush administration used this old method to divert the attention of Americans away from their ...

...failure to find Osama bin Laden...

...or questions about who bought Bush's stock in Harken Energy (in what had the appearance of a potential insider trading scandal)...

...or the numerous charges against Cheney of conflicts of interest...

...hiding the pervasive influence of energy industry executives in shaping U.S. energy policy...

...and Halliburton's documented shenanigans while he was CEO*,

...or the plunge of working class wealth to levels not seen since the Great Depression.

*During Cheney's tenure, Halliburton increased their overseas tax havens from 9 to 44, thereby decreasing their tax liability from $302 million in 1998 to an $85 million refund the following year. The Securities Exchange Commission is investigating whether Halliburton artificially inflated revenue by $234 million during that time. Source: "Cheney, Halliburton and the Spoils of War" by Lee Drutman and Charlie Cray (of Citizen Works), www.CorpWatch.org

But that seemingly obvious ploy is only the second level of a three-level illusion.

Behind the war talk, and behind the "it's a diversion" talk, the real trick is being carried out.

The real agenda, relentlessly moving forward with hardly a notice in corporate-owned media and hardly a peep from corporate-owned politicians, is the dismantling of democracy.

As the administration's foreign misadventures continue to impact us daily, Americans are now beginning to wake up to the fact that the real war is being waged here at home.

Aw..

Hey!

It is, however, a confused awakening.

?

For example, Americans wonder why the Bush administration seems so intent on crippling local, state, and federal governments by starving them of funds and, at the same time, creating a huge annual federal deficit — on the order of $500 billion —

Grrr...

DEFICIT

— thanks in part to the $6 billion monthly cost of operations in Iraq...

...and because of huge tax cuts for the wealthy.

Bush's behavior has even caught the attention of the International Monetary Fund, which has warned about the risks to the U.S. economy of accumulating such a staggering debt.

Worst of all, our children will have to repay this borrowing.

But it's my allowance!

Many think it's just to fund tax cuts and subsidies for the rich, that the multimillionaire CEOs who've taken over virtually all senior posts in the Bush administration are just pigs at the trough, and this is a spectacular but ordinary form of self-serving corruption. It all seems so plausible, and there's even a grain of truth to it.

But juicy deals for Bush administration insiders are just a by-product of the real and deeper war against democracy.

The conservatives are perfectly happy for us to think that they're just opportunists skirting the edges of legality and morality, but this is far more dangerous than simple government corruption.

HA! HA! HA!

Oh! How quaint!

...and then he called me greedy!

Indeed, the conservatives profess to being anti-government.

As influential tax-cut advocate and spokesman for the conservative agenda Grover Norquist told National Public Radio's Mara Liasson in a May 25, 2001, Morning Edition interview...

"I don't want to abolish government. I simply want to reduce it to the size where I can drag it into the bathroom and drown it in the bathtub."

Without a larger view, the issues of

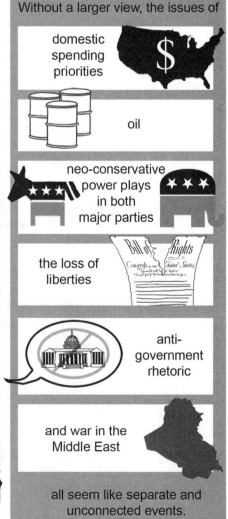

domestic spending priorities

oil

neo-conservative power plays in both major parties

the loss of liberties

anti-government rhetoric

and war in the Middle East

all seem like separate and unconnected events.

The "new conservatives" who've seized the Republican Party and (through the Democratic Leadership Council [DLC]) are nipping at the heels of the Democratic Party are not our parents' conservatives.

They're not.

Hmmm... you don't look familiar...

Historic conservatives like former U.S. Senator Barry Goldwater and ex-Presidents Harry Truman and Dwight Eisenhower would be appalled.

GASP!

Although the conservatives' philosophical roots go back to Alexander Hamilton, who openly argued during the Constitutional Convention that royalty was the best form of government...

...they have mostly been on the fringe, nipping at the heels of democracy.

What we are seeing now, in the conservative agenda, is nothing less than an attempt to over-throw republican democracy...

OW!

...and replace it with a worldwide feudal state.

The last time this happened, the feudalists took over a monarchy and then North America.

In December 1600, Queen Elizabeth I chartered the East India Company, ultimately leading to a corporate takeover of the Americas...

...that the colonists ended with the Boston Tea Party...

...and, three years later, the American Revolution.

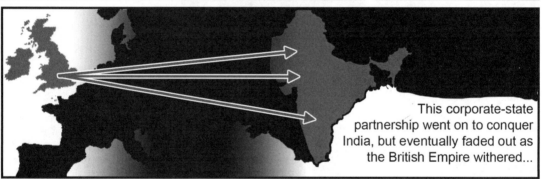

This corporate-state partnership went on to conquer India, but eventually faded out as the British Empire withered...

...and the British government, along with most of Western Europe, embraced Jeffersonian forms of democracy.

But it raised its head again in the 20th Century, revived by Hitler, Mussolini, and Franco.

Since the "Reagan Revolution," two centuries after we rose up and rebelled against King George III for his support of corporate feudalism in Boston Harbor, this ancient enemy of democracy is again trying to seize America.

Reagan ignored the Sherman Act and other restraints on corporations, and sold at fire-sale prices the airwaves once held in common by We the People.

The result was predictable: a merger and acquisitions frenzy, and the takeover of American media by a handful of mega-corporations.

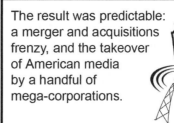

Bill Clinton then helped export corporatism to the industrialized world when he pushed legislation through Congress to authorize the GATT/WTO* agreements...

...which have fueled a rampant globalization that has contributed to the trampling of world-wide environmental protections...

STOMP!

...continuing exploitation of workers and other citizens of Third World countries...

...and greater clout for transnational corporations.

Thus, the war on Iraq was just one front in the larger feudal war against democracy itself. (And a particularly useful one. It gave the corporate feudal lords access to vast oil wealth...

...and was so effective at distracting the populace from Bush's outrageous domestic agenda that we might expect to see a similar "crisis" dominating the news once more.)

Can they really get away with that... again?

*General Agreement on Tariffs and Trade and the World Trade Organization. See Appendix A for globalization links.

That's the big question, isn't it?

The conservatives are in control now, and they are not going to go quietly. But the choice — of how we're governed, of how America interrelates with the rest of the world —

— is still ours.

It sure doesn't feel like it.

These are long, historical dynamics unfolding — two clashing fundamental views of who we are as humans and our role in the natural order of Life.

Years before America turned its attention to fighting fascism in Germany, President Roosevelt was concerned about the rise of a corporate feudalism here in the United States. In a speech in Philadelphia on June 27, 1936, he said:

"Out of this modern civilization, economic royalists carved new dynasties. New kingdoms were built upon concentration of control over material things. Through new uses of corporations, banks and securities, new machinery of industry and agriculture, of labor and capital — all undreamed of by the Fathers — the whole structure of modern life was impressed into this royal service."

Roosevelt suggested that human nature may play a part in it all, but that didn't make it tolerable.

"It was natural and perhaps human that the privileged princes of these new economic dynasties, thirsting for power, reached out for control over government itself."

"As a result, **the average man once more confronts the problem that faced the Minute Man.**"

Republicans of the day lashed out in the press and on radio, charging that Roosevelt was anti-American, even communist.

Without a moment's hesitation, he threw it back in their faces...

"These economic royalists complain that we seek to overthrow the institutions of America,"

...Roosevelt thundered in that 1936 speech.

"What they really complain of is that we seek to take away their power. Our allegiance to American institutions **requires the overthrow of this kind of power.** In vain they seek to hide behind the flag and the Constitution. In their blindness they forget what the flag and the Constitution stand for."

Those of us who still believe in republican democracy would have We the People make the decisions through representatives we've elected ...

...without the feudal influence of corporate money.

We realize that "big government" is, indeed, a menace when it's no longer responsive to its own people, as happened in Germany and Russia in the last century and is happening today in America under the neo-conservatives.

But we also remember the vision of a free and democratic America: a sacred archetype so powerful that freedom fighters in Beijing's Tiananmen Square marched to their deaths carrying a 36-foot-tall papier mâché replica of the Statue of Liberty while quoting the words of Thomas Jefferson.

51

THE CONSERVATIVE AGENDA

When you look closely, you discover that what so many are calling the "conservative agenda" would be shocking and alien to historic conservatives like Republicans Goldwater, Eisenhower and Teddy Roosevelt.

It really has nothing to do with

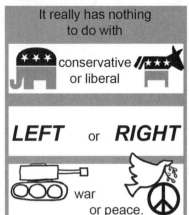

conservative or liberal

LEFT or **RIGHT**

war or peace.

It doesn't really care about

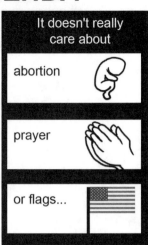

abortion

prayer

or flags...

...although these are useful props to bring in fringe groups to "fill the big tent."

PARTY RALLY

PICK YOUR ISSUE!

It's not even about liberty, freedom, or prosperity.

Bill of Rights

Congress of the United States,

Today's so-called "conservative agenda" is, very simply, about **ownership**.

Specifically, ownership of the assets of the United States of America — things previously owned by We the People.

Constitution

Ultimately, it is about ownership of the United States government itself.

Here's how it works...

 In a democracy there are some things we all own together.

Often referred to as "the Commons," they include the necessities and commonalities of life:

our air

water

septic systems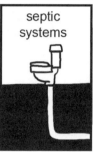

transportation routes

educational systems

radio and TV spectrums

...and — in every developed nation in the world except America —

the nation's health care system.

But the most important of the Commons in a democracy is the government itself.

The Founders' idea of a democratic republic was to create a common institution owned by its own citizens, answerable to its own citizens, and authorized to exist and continue existing solely "by the consent of the governed."

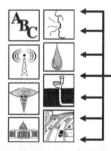 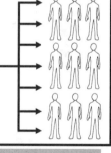

As the prescient Chief Justice of Wisconsin's Supreme Court, Edward G. Ryan, said ominously in his 1873 speech to the graduating class of the University of Wisconsin Law School:

"[There] is looming up a new and dark power. ... The enterprises of the country are aggregating vast corporate combinations of unexampled capital, boldly marching, not for economical conquests only, but for political power. ... The question will arise and arise in your day, though perhaps not fully in mine, **which shall rule — wealth or man**; which shall lead — money or intellect; who shall fill public stations — **educated and patriotic freemen**, or the **feudal serfs of corporate capital**."

Make no mistake —democracy itself is at risk as we enter a new and unknown, but hauntingly familiar, era.

It's new because it represents a virtual abandonment of the egalitarian and democratic archetypes the founders of the United States put into place in our Constitution and Bill of Rights.

And it's hauntingly familiar because it resembles in many ways one of the most stable and long-term of all social structures to have ever established itself in the modern history of civilization: feudalism.

Feudalism?

Yes.

Let's be blunt...

The real agenda of the new conservatives is nothing less than the destruction of democracy in the United States of America.

And feudalism is one of their weapons.

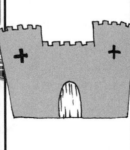

Their rallying cry is that government is the enemy...

54

...and thus must be "drowned in a bathtub."

In that, they've mistaken our government for the former Soviet Union, or confused novelist Ayn Rand's fictional and disintegrating America for the real thing.

Wait! What country am I in??

The government of the United States is *us*.

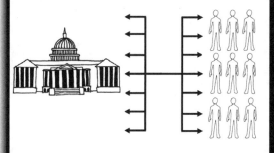

It was designed to be a government of, by, and for We the People.

It's not an enemy to be destroyed; it's a means by which we administer and preserve the Commons that we collectively own.

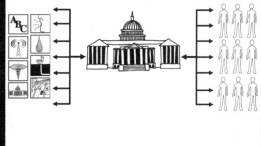

Nonetheless, the new conservatives see our democratic government as the enemy.

And if they plan to destroy democracy, they must have something in mind to replace it with.

In the conservatives' brave new world, corporations are more suited to governance than are the unpredictable rabble called citizens.

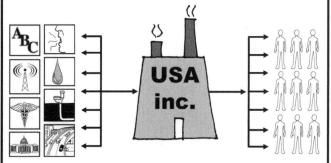

Corporations should control politics, the Commons, health care, our airwaves, the "free" market, and even our schools.

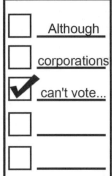

Although

corporations

✓ can't vote...

_____

_____

...these new conservatives claim they should have human rights...

...like privacy from government inspections of their political activity...

...and the free speech right to lie to politicians and citizens in PR and advertising.

A

B

Although corporations don't need to breathe fresh air or drink pure water, these new conservatives would hand over to them the power to self-regulate poisonous emissions into our air and water.

While these new conservatives claim corporations should have the rights of persons, they don't mind if corporations use hostile financial force to take over other, smaller corporations in a bizarre form of corporate slavery called monopoly.

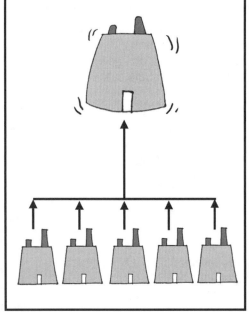

Corporations can't die, so aren't subject to inheritance taxes or probate.

RIP   RIP

They can't be put in prison, so even when they cause death they are only subject to fines.

You sound sort of anti-business.

Not at all!

In fact, I'm a businessman, myself. I've started several corporations, and want such small enterprises to continue to flourish. And, I'm very much for democracy — the most difficult and wondrous political experiment the developed world has ever seen.

But, most of us don't realize that it's now being stolen from us, right under our noses.

Let's look at how this is happening.

Corporations and their CEOs are America's new feudal lords, and the new conservatives are their obliging servants and mouthpieces.

The conservative mantra is:

"Less government!"

But the dirty little secret of the new conservatives is that just as nature abhors a vacuum, so also do politics and power.

Every time government of, by, and for We the People is pushed out of administering some part of this nation's vast Commons, corporations step in.

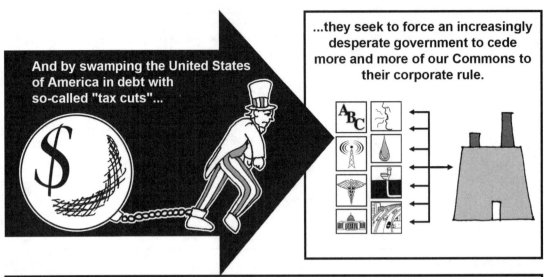

And by swamping the United States of America in debt with so-called "tax cuts"...

...they seek to force an increasingly desperate government to cede more and more of our Commons to their corporate rule.

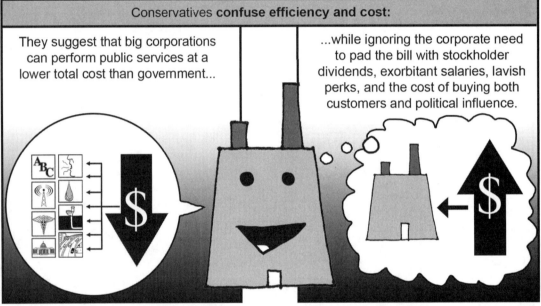

Conservatives confuse efficiency and cost:

They suggest that big corporations can perform public services at a lower total cost than government...

...while ignoring the corporate need to pad the bill with stockholder dividends, exorbitant salaries, lavish perks, and the cost of buying both customers and political influence.

They want to frame this as the solution of the "free market," and talk about entrepreneurs and small businesses filling up the holes left when government lets go of public property.

LOCAL STORE

But these are straw man arguments.

What they are really advocating is corporate rule...

...and, ultimately, a feudal state controlled exclusively by the largest of the corporations.

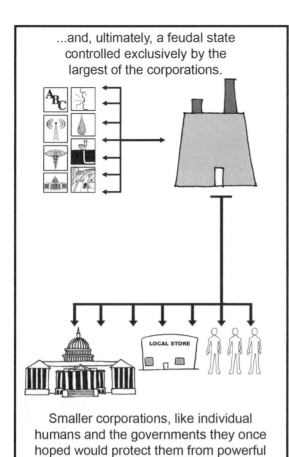

Smaller corporations, like individual humans and the governments they once hoped would protect them from powerful feudal forces, can watch but they can't play.

The roots of this struggle go deep. In his lecture "Angloam," the great 19th century transcendental philosopher Ralph Waldo Emerson told us that in America...

"the old contest of feudalism and democracy renews itself here on a new battlefield."

The modern-day conservative movement goes back to the beginnings of the Republic and Federalists like Alexander Hamilton and John Adams...

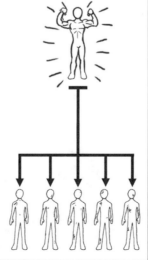

...who argued that for a society to be stable it must have a governing elite, and this elite must be separate both in power and privilege from what Adams referred to as "the rabble."

Their Federalist party imploded in the early 19th Century...

POP!

...in large part because of public revulsion over Federalist elitism, a symptom of which was Adams' signing of the Alien and Sedition Acts.

If you've read only the Republican biographies of John Adams, you probably don't remember these laws, even though they were the biggest thing to have happened in Adams' entire four years in office and the reason why the citizens of America voted him out of office...

...and voted in Jefferson — who loudly and publicly opposed the Acts.

They were a 1797 version of the Patriot Act and Patriot II, with startlingly similar language. I'll tell this story later.

Destroyed by their embrace of this early form of despotism, the Federalists were replaced first in the early 1800s by the short-lived Whigs and then, starting with Lincoln, by the modern-day Republicans...

...who, after Lincoln's death, firmly staked out their ancestral Federalist position as the party of wealthy corporate and private interests.

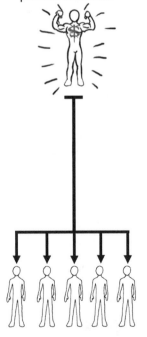

And now, under the disguise of the word "conservative" (classical conservatives are rolling in their graves), these old-time feudalists have nearly completed their takeover of our great nation.

Feudalism doesn't refer to a point in time or history when streets were filled with mud and people lived as peasants (although that was sometimes the case).

Instead, it refers to an economic and political system, just like "democracy" or "communism" or "socialism" or "theocracy."

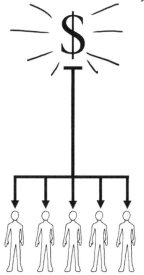

In a feudal state, those who own the greatest wealth hold power.

At its essential core, feudalism could be defined as "government of, by, and for the rich."

Marc Bloch is one of the great 20th century scholars of the feudal history of Europe. In his book *Feudal Society*, he points out that feudalism is a fracturing of one authoritarian hierarchical structure into another. The state disintegrates, as unelected but wealthy power brokers take over.

In almost every case — in Europe, China, South America, and Japan —

— Bloch notes that...

"feudalism coincided with a profound weakening of the State, particularly in its protective capacity."

Normally, feudal societies don't emerge in civilizations with a strong social safety net and a proactive government.

Though there is a slight debate among scholars, the consensus is that **when the wealthiest in a society take over government and then weaken it so it no longer can represent the interests of the people, the transition has begun into a new era of feudalism.**

"European feudalism should therefore be seen as the outcome of the violent dissolution of older societies," **Bloch says.**

Whether the agent of power and wealth that takes the place of government is a local baron, lord, king, or corporation...

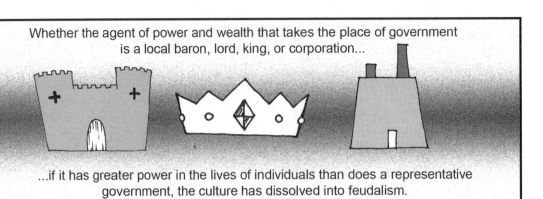

...if it has greater power in the lives of individuals than does a representative government, the culture has dissolved into feudalism.

Bluntly, Bloch states:

"The feudal system meant the rigorous economic subjection of a host of humble folk to a few powerful men."

This doesn't mean the end of government but, instead, the subordination of government to the interests of the feudal lords.

Interestingly, even in feudal Europe, Bloch points out,

"The concept of the State never absolutely disappeared, and where it retained the most vitality, men continued to call themselves 'free.'"

The transition from a governmental society to a feudal one is marked by the rapid accumulation of power and wealth in a few hands...

...with a corresponding reduction in the power and responsibilities of government.

Once the rich and powerful gain control of the government, they turn it upon itself, usually first eliminating its taxation process as it applies to themselves.

Says Bloch:

"Nobles need not pay taille [taxes]."

Bringing us back to the present, consider that in 1982, just before the Reagan-Bush "supply side" tax cut, the average wealth of individuals on the Forbes 400 list was $200 million.

200 Million

1982

Just four years later, their average wealth was $500 million each, aided by massive tax cuts.

500 Million

1986

200 Million

1982

In the Bush administration's tax cuts, the top one percent of income earners receives over thirty-seven percent of the cuts.

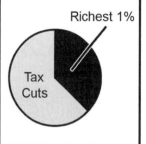

Richest 1%

Tax Cuts

Those statistics are even more shocking when you consider that the richest one percent of Americans now owns as much wealth as the bottom ninety-five percent.

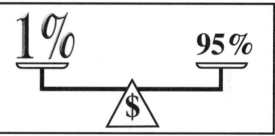

1%   95%

$

Those who would take over the government of the United States have a specific plan. It begins with tax cuts...

...which are then followed by handing government-mandated services over to private corporations.

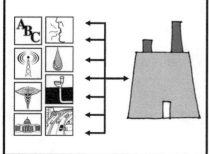

Tax cuts are not just about kowtowing to the nobles of the new conservative feudal state.

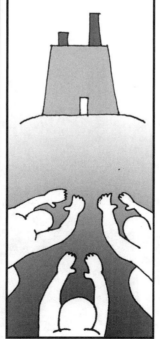

The most important function of tax cuts is to **deprive government of oxygen.**

URK!

63

The result is that the **government must then turn to private corporations — the new feudal lords — to administer the Commons.**

The transfer of the Commons ranges from:

health care for the elderly

to the vote

...as we're seeing now with private corporations linked to hard-right Republicans taking over the election systems of states like Georgia, Florida, and Texas.

According to hard-right Republicans, killing off government to make way for corporate rule is truly at the core of the so-called "conservative agenda." Remember the infamous Grover Norquist and his intentions for democracy?

At first, gullible politicians and voters thought drowning a democratic government in the bathtub was, at worst, just another way for big business to make more money.

It might even make some of the functions of government more efficient, they thought...

...even though any benefits of that efficiency would be turned over to stockholders and CEOs rather than the broader public that uses the Commons.

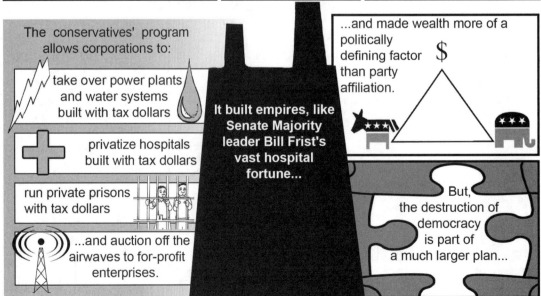

The conservatives' program allows corporations to:

take over power plants and water systems built with tax dollars

privatize hospitals built with tax dollars

run private prisons with tax dollars

...and auction off the airwaves to for-profit enterprises.

It built empires, like Senate Majority leader Bill Frist's vast hospital fortune...

...and made wealth more of a politically defining factor $ than party affiliation.

But, the destruction of democracy is part of a much larger plan...

THE LOSS OF THE COMMONS

The Bush Administration plan to privatize parts of Medicare represents just one thread in the larger fabric of an insidious New World Order.

They're hoping that Americans won't notice.

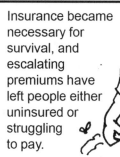

The transformation of healthcare into a for-profit industry has led to spiraling costs (and millions of dollars for Bill Frist and his ilk) –

– ballooning to $1.4 trillion annually, far and away the largest single "industry" in the American economy.

Insurance became necessary for survival, and escalating premiums have left people either uninsured or struggling to pay.

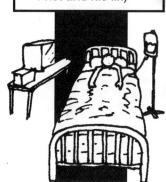

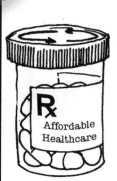

The Clinton administration was prepared to answer the concern of the majority of Americans who supported national health care.

But that would harm corporate profits.

I've got some real concerns about national health care.

So do I. But, whenever the issue comes up, the conservatives ask over and over again, "Do you want government bureaucrats deciding which doctor you can see?"

As a yes/no question, the answer is pretty simple for most Americans:

NO!

But, as is so often the case when conservatives try to influence public opinion, the true issue isn't honestly stated.

The real question is:

Do you want government bureaucrats (who are answerable to elected officials and thus subject to the will of We the People) making decisions about your healthcare, or would you rather have corporate bureaucrats (who are answerable only to their boards and CEOs and work in a profit-driven environment) making decisions about your healthcare?

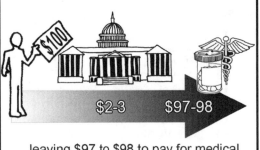

For every $100 that passes through the hands of the government-administered Medicare programs, between $2 and $3 is spent on administration...

$2-3 $97-98

...leaving $97 to $98 to pay for medical services and drugs.

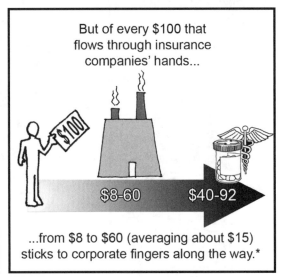

But of every $100 that flows through insurance companies' hands...

$8-60 $40-92

...from $8 to $60 (averaging about $15) sticks to corporate fingers along the way.*

*New England Journal of Medicine, August 2003.

Thus, an industry is born: profiting in the expanding definition of "crime" (especially in the dubious "War on Drugs," which now yields 50% of all U.S. prisoners*)...

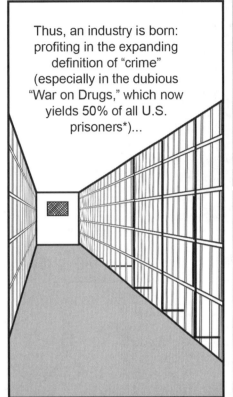

...the expansion of the number of apprehended criminals...

...and incarceration of more of them for longer and longer periods of time via mandatory sentencing laws.

The U.S. is now the world leader among industrialized nations in citizens who are locked up.**

There is little incentive for rehabilitation or to implement proven programs to reduce recidivism, because a high rate of prisoners returning to prison is highly profitable.

Warehousing people becomes no different than growing chickens or cows in cages or stalls.

There do not have to be quaint moral, ethical or practical social considerations, because it's just business.

The bottom line rules.

*Up from 17% in 1970.
**In the U.S. in 2001, there were 6.6 million people in jail or prison, on parole or probation – a number that has *quadrupled* since 1978.

On the other hand, having government protect the quality of the nation's air and water by mandating pollution controls doesn't enhance corporate profits.

Neither does instituting a more efficient, single-payer healthcare system...

...nor does restricting monopoly control of local media markets.

While the government still holds most of the keys to the riches of the Commons held in trust for us all...

...corporations are intent on converting these public riches into private profit.

For example, in an NPR *Morning Edition* report, Rick Carr said...

"Current FCC* chair Michael Powell says he has faith the market will provide. What's more, he says he'd rather have the market decide than government."

In this, Powell was reciting the conservative mantra.

Misconstruing 18th century economist Adam Smith (who actually warned about the dangers of the invisible hand of the marketplace trampling the rights and needs of the people)...

...Powell suggests that business always knows best.

Trust me!

The market will decide.

Bigger isn't badder.

*Federal Communications Commission

But experience shows that the very competition that conservatives claim to embrace is destroyed by the unrestrained growth of corporate interests.

It's called monopoly.

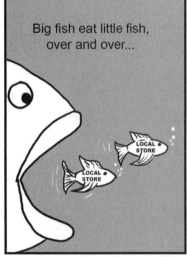

Big fish eat little fish, over and over...

LOCAL STORE
LOCAL STORE

...until there are no little fish left.

Look at the thoroughfares of any American city and ask yourself how many of the businesses there are locally owned.

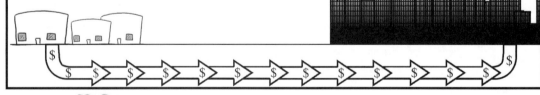

Instead of cash circulating within a local and competitive economy, at midnight every night a button is pushed and the local money is vacuumed away to New York, Chicago or Bentonville, Arkansas.

$ $ $ $ $ $ $ $ $ $ $ $ $ $ $

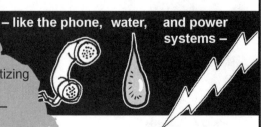

What little planning the Bush administration did for post-invasion Iraq focused on privatizing their government resources –

– like the phone, water, and power systems –

– and particularly the highly lucrative oil industry.

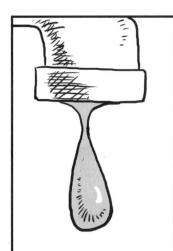

The public resource that is perhaps the most coveted now is water. The increasing scarcity of fresh water supplies is revealing the true value of this essential element –

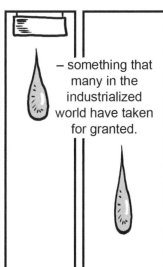

– something that many in the industrialized world have taken for granted.

No longer.

In the 21st century, water will be the most precious commodity on the planet –

– more so than oil...

...or electricity.

The transnational mega-corporations have water in their sights.

A subsidiary of the infamous Enron corporation was in the process of capturing major water rights from Florida (Gov. Jeb Bush territory!) as part of Florida's Everglades restoration project...

...when Enron's spiraling financial troubles scuttled the attempt.

The World Bank and International Monetary Fund have been colluding with transnationals to push countries with struggling economies into privatization schemes, many with disastrous results.

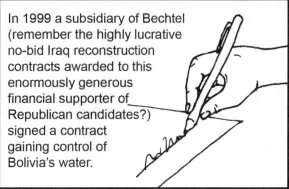

In 1999 a subsidiary of Bechtel (remember the highly lucrative no-bid Iraq reconstruction contracts awarded to this enormously generous financial supporter of Republican candidates?) signed a contract gaining control of Bolivia's water.

The government acquiesced to this sweetheart deal as a requirement by the World Bank for receiving a $25 million loan.

With their partners, Bechtel paid out less than $20,000 for a public water system worth millions.

Their projected annual income was $58 million.

Rates were quickly increased — from 100 to 200%.*

Some families were paying 20-50% of their monthly income for water.

The Bolivian government declared all water in Bolivia corporate property.

Legally, no one was supposed to draw water from a well or collect rainwater without financial obligation to the new "owner."

The people responded.

A four-day general strike in January 2000 provoked a violent police response and the imposition of martial law.

Another seven days of wide-spread, organized protests and civil disobedience in April forced the country's president to terminate the contract.

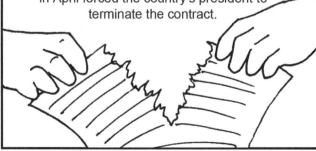

*www.citizen.org

Just as the kings and nobles of old sucked dry the resources of the people they claimed to own, these examples represent feudalism in its most raw and naked form.

It is in these arguments of the modern conservative movement for unrestrained corporatism that we see the naked face of Hamilton's Federalists.

It's the face of wealth and privilege — what Jefferson called a "pseudo-aristocracy" —

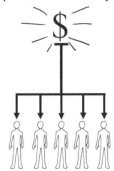

—that works to its own enrichment and gain regardless of the harm done to the nation, the Commons, or the "We the People" rabble.

It is, in its most complete form, the face that would "drown government in a bathtub"...

That sneers at the First Amendment by putting up isolated "free speech zones" for protesters...

That openly and harshly suggests that those who are poor, unemployed, or underemployed are suffering from character defects.

That works hard to protect the corporate interest...

...but is happy to ignore the public interest.

Mmf! Mmf!

That says it doesn't matter what happens to the humans living in what a national conservative talk show host laughingly calls "turd world nations."

These new conservatives would have us trade in our democracy for a "corporatocracy," a form of feudal government most recently reinvented by Mussolini* when he recommended a "merger of business and state interests" as a way of creating a government that would be invincibly strong.

Mussolini called it fascism.

Media and other corporations will suck up to government when they think they can get regulations that will enhance their profits.

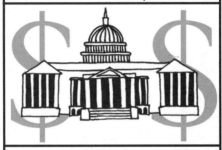

We see this daily in the halls of Congress and in the lobbying efforts directed at our regulatory agencies.

We see it in the millions of dollars in trips and gifts given to FCC commissioners, which in another era would have been called bribes.

These corporate-embracing conservatives are not working for what's best for democracy...

...for America...

...or for the interests of We the People.

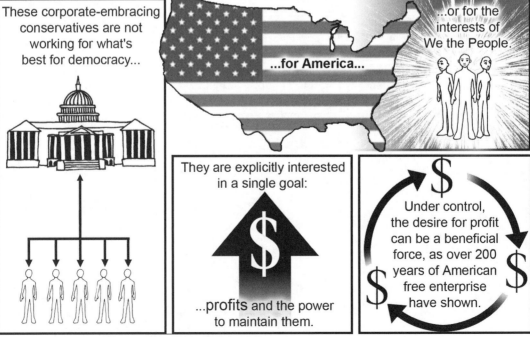

They are explicitly interested in a single goal:

...profits and the power to maintain them.

Under control, the desire for profit can be a beneficial force, as over 200 years of American free enterprise have shown.

*Mussolini ruled Italy from the 1920s till his death in 1945.

But unrestrained, as billionaire financial wizard and philanthropist George Soros warns us so eloquently, it will create monopolies and destroy democracy.

The new conservatives are systematically dismantling our governmental systems of checks and balances...

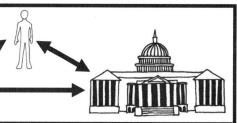

Mmf!

...for considering the public good when regulating private corporate behavior...

...and protecting those individuals, small businesses, and local communities who are unable to protect themselves from giant corporate predators.

LOCAL STORE

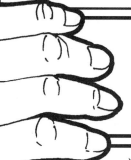

They want to replace government of, by, and for We the People, with a corporate feudal state, turning America's citizens into their vassals and serfs.

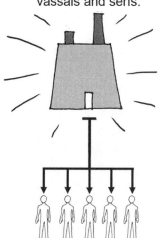

I don't understand how this could happen in this country.

Well, the battle to control American democracy certainly goes back to the Federalists and the beginning of the republic, but you really need to understand the railroad barons of the late 19th century in order to realize how skillfully the forces of corporate feudalism have chipped away at the marvelous political system America's Founders created.

THE RAILROAD BARONS RETURN

The railroad barons first tried to infiltrate the halls of government in the early years after the Civil War.

The efforts of these men brought the Ulysses Grant administration into such disrepute, as a result of what were then called "the railroad bribery scandals," that Grant's own Republican party refused to re-nominate him for the third term he wanted and ran Rutherford B. Hayes instead.

Although their misbehaviors with the administration and Congress were exposed, the railroad barons still represented the most powerful corporations in America, and they were incredibly tenacious.

They mounted challenge after challenge before the Supreme Court, claiming that the 14th Amendment should grant the railroads human rights under the Bill of Rights.

Finally, in 1886, they pulled off a coup.

In 1886, Santa Clara County, California, sued the Southern Pacific Railroad over non-payment of taxes and, in losing the lawsuit, paved the way for the corporate takeover of the United States of America.

On appeal, the U.S. Supreme Court ruled that the state tax assessor, not the county assessor, had the right to determine the taxable value of fence posts along the railroad's right-of-way.

Before the Supreme Court hearing was held, the railroad — apparently not willing to rely merely on the strength of its arguments — had courted Justice Stephen Field with, among other things, the possibility of support for a presidential run.

In the National Archives, we found letters from the railroads offering free trips and other benefits to the 1886 Court's Chief Justice, Morrison R. Waite.

To top that off, one of their own was the Court Reporter, a highly prestigious position in those days, with a salary even higher than that of the justices themselves.

The railroad argued that the Fourteenth Amendment — which freed the slaves in 1868 by guaranteeing all persons equal protection under the law regardless of race —

About time!

Bill of Rights
Congress of the United States

— had also freed corporations because they should be considered "persons" just like humans.

Party Crasher.

Hey guys!

The attorney for Santa Clara County, Delphin M. Delmas, fought back ferociously.

"The shield behind which [the Southern Pacific Railroad] attacks the Constitution and laws of California is the Fourteenth Amendment,"

...said Delmas before the Supreme Court...

"It argues that the amendment guarantees to every person within the jurisdiction of the State the equal protection of the laws; that a corporation is a person; that, therefore, it must receive the same protection as that accorded to all other persons in like circumstances."

The entire idea was beyond the pale, Delmas said. He told the court...

"The whole history of the Fourteenth Amendment demonstrates beyond dispute that its whole scope and object was to establish equality between men — an attainable result — and not to establish equality between natural and artificial beings — an impossible result."

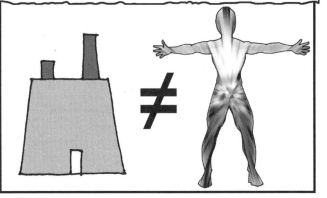

The purpose of the Fourteenth Amendment, passed just after the Civil War, was clear, Delmas said.

Amendment to
the Constitution

"Its mission was to raise the humble, the down-trodden, and the oppressed to the level of the most exalted upon the broad plane of humanity — to make man the equal of man; but not to make the creature of the State — the bodiless, soulless, and mystic creature called a corporation — the equal of the creature of God."

Delmas had every reason to assume the Court would agree with him — it already had in several similar cases.

For example, in 1873, one of the first Supreme Court rulings on the Fourteenth Amendment, which had passed only five years earlier, involved not slaves but the railroads.

Justice Samuel F. Miller minced no words in chastising corporations for trying to claim the rights of human beings. In the majority opinion, he wrote that the amendment's...

..."one pervading purpose was the freedom of the slave race, the security and firm establishment of that freedom, and the protection of the newly-made freeman and citizen from the oppression of those who had formerly exercised unlimited dominion over him."

In the end, Chief Justice Waite didn't give in to the railroad's arguments and pressures in Santa Clara County v. Southern Pacific R.R. Co.

He refused to rule that the railroad corporations were persons in the same category as humans.

In a handwritten note Waite wrote:

"We avoided meeting the constitutional question in the decision."

And nowhere in the decision itself does the Court say corporations are persons.

However, in writing up the case's headnote — a commentary that has no precedential status — the Court's reporter, a former railroad president named J.C. Bancroft Davis, defied his own Chief Justice and improperly opened the headnote with the sentence:

"The defendant Corporations are persons within the intent of the clause in section 1 of the Fourteen Amendment to the Constitution of the United States, which forbids a State to deny to any person within its jurisdiction the equal protection of the laws."

By the time the Reporter's headnotes were published, the Chief Justice was dead.

Quickly, corporate attorneys picked up the language of Davis's headnote and began to recite it like a mantra.

"Corporations are persons"

"Corporations are persons"

"Corporations are persons"

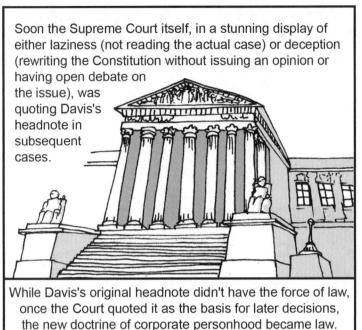

Soon the Supreme Court itself, in a stunning display of either laziness (not reading the actual case) or deception (rewriting the Constitution without issuing an opinion or having open debate on the issue), was quoting Davis's headnote in subsequent cases.

While Davis's original headnote didn't have the force of law, once the Court quoted it as the basis for later decisions, the new doctrine of corporate personhood became law.

Wasn't that an awfully big leap?

SAFE JOBS

It sure was!

America's Founders were clear when they wrote the Bill of Rights that humans had rights...

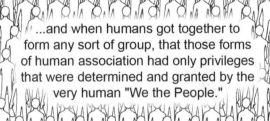

...and when humans got together to form any sort of group, that those forms of human association had only privileges that were determined and granted by the very human "We the People."

But, as if by magic, the Court's reporter effectively rewrote the American Constitution at the behest of the railroad barons...

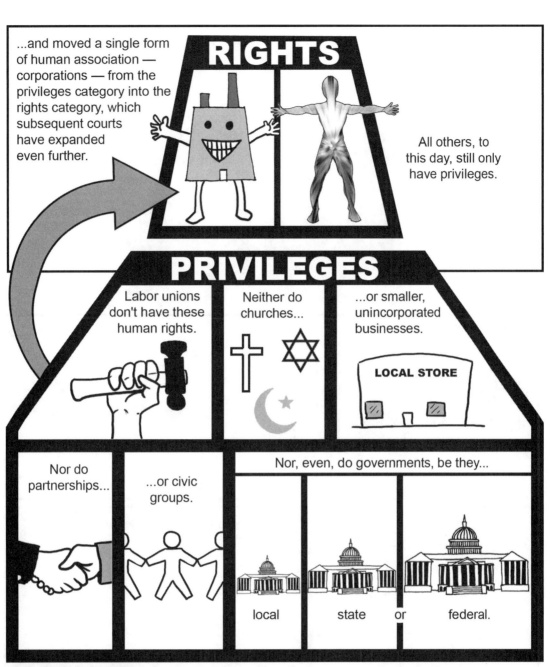

...and moved a single form of human association — corporations — from the privileges category into the rights category, which subsequent courts have expanded even further.

RIGHTS

All others, to this day, still only have privileges.

PRIVILEGES

Labor unions don't have these human rights.

Neither do churches...

...or smaller, unincorporated businesses.

LOCAL STORE

Nor do partnerships...

...or civic groups.

Nor, even, do governments, be they...

local   state   or   federal.

Now, individual citizen voters must compete with corporations on unequal footing.

Kind of a raw deal isn't it?

Some have thought so.

When the Constitution and Bill of Rights were submitted for ratification, Jefferson and Madison proposed an 11th Amendment that would not only make it illegal for corporations to own other corporations...

...but would also ban them from giving money to politicians...

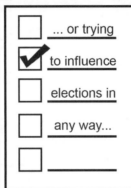

... or trying
✓ to influence
elections in
any way...
_____

...restrict corporations to a single business purpose...

MISSION

...limit the lifetime of a corporation to something roughly similar to that of productive humans (20 to 40 years back then)...

R.I.P.

Bob Corp
1787-1827

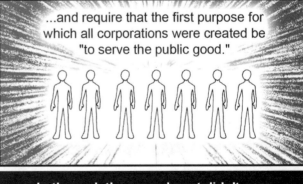

...and require that the first purpose for which all corporations were created be "to serve the public good."

In the end, the amendment didn't pass because many argued it was unnecessary:

Virtually all states already had such laws on the books from the founding of this nation until the Age of the Robber Barons.

STATE GOVT.

PRIVILEGES

But, corporations grew, and began to flex their muscle.

Politicians who believed in republican democracy were alarmed by the possibility of a new feudalism, a state run by and for the benefit of powerful private interests.

President Andrew Jackson, in an 1830s speech to Congress, said...

"The question is ... whether the people of the United States are to govern through representatives chosen by their unbiased suffrages [votes] or whether the **money and power of a great corporation** are to be secretly **exerted to influence their judgment and control their decisions**."

And the president who followed him, Martin Van Buren, added in his annual address to Congress...

"I am more than ever convinced of the dangers to which the free and unbiased exercise of political opinion — the only sure foundation and safeguard of republican government — would be exposed by any further increase of the already **overgrown influence of corporate authorities**."

In April 1906, Theodore Roosevelt looked at the situation and bluntly observed...

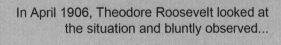

"Behind the ostensible government sits enthroned an **invisible government** owing no allegiance and acknowledging no responsibility to the people. To destroy this invisible government, to befoul the **unholy alliance between corrupt business and corrupt politics** is the first task of the statesmanship of the day."

THEY'RE BACK!

Today, the conservatives are set to complete what the railroad barons pushed the Grant administration to start: to take democracy and its institutions of governance...

...which the Founders fought and died for...

...from the hands of the human citizens/voters.

YOINK!

Hey!

They are handing control to the very types of monopolistic corporations the Founders fought against when they led the Tea Party revolt against the East India Company in Boston Harbor in 1773.

Here are just a few egregious examples:

In June 2003, despite protests from millions of Americans, corporate-friendly Michael Powell's FCC lifted some of the last tattered restrictions on media ownership...

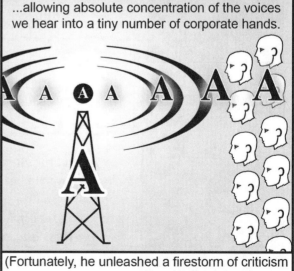

...allowing absolute concentration of the voices we hear into a tiny number of corporate hands.

(Fortunately, he unleashed a firestorm of criticism from conservatives, moderates and liberals in Congress, who vowed to re-close the floodgates.)

84

On another front, a major multinational corporation has claimed the right to deceive people in its PR as its 1st Amendment right of free speech.

The New York Times Corporation editorialized in support.

Even the ACLU*, unable to see the forest for the trees, adopted a misguided advocacy, seeking to preserve First Amendment rights even for "those" (corporations), who don't legitimately warrant them.

Bill of Rights

Congress of the United States,

In addition, as much as half the federal workforce is slated to be replaced by corporate workers...

...under a new Bush edict.

Government — which doesn't have constitutional human rights of privacy, and so is answerable to We the People —

— will then be able to use Fourth Amendment rights of privacy to hide what those workers do and how they do it from the prying eyes of citizens and voters.

In a similar fashion, corporate-owned and thus unaccountable-to-the-people voting machines are being installed nationwide.

In the last election these machines often produced vote results so different from exit polls that pollsters who have been successfully calling elections for over 50 years threw up their hands and closed shop.

CLOSED

*American Civil Liberties Union

85

And, in the ultimate irony...

Let's take this baby for a ride!

...the man in charge of the Bush administration's economic policy, Secretary of the Treasury John Snow, is a multi-millionaire campaign contributor, chairman of the Business Roundtable (an elite corps of 100 of the nation's most powerful corporate CEOs) and, himself, a railroad baron.

That sucks!

Yeah it does!

You bet. It's a sorry state of affairs. And, it shouldn't be that way.

Corporations are created by humans to further the goal of making money.

And, as engineer, architect and writer Buckminster Fuller said in his brilliant essay, *Grunch of Giants...*

"Corporations are neither physical nor metaphysical phenomena. They are socio-economic ploys — legally enacted game-playing."

Corporations are non-living, non-breathing, legal fictions.

They feel no pain.

TINK

They don't need clean water to drink...

...fresh air to breathe...

...or healthy food to consume.

They can live forever.

RIP RIP

They can't be put in prison.

They can change their identity or appearance in a day...

...change their citizenship in an hour...

Surname
BOB CORP.

Nationality
ANYWHERE

Residency
EVERYWHERE

...rip off parts of themselves and create entirely new entities.

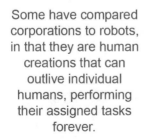

Some have compared corporations to robots, in that they are human creations that can outlive individual humans, performing their assigned tasks forever.

Hey Bro!

BEEP Don't insult me.

Scientist and prolific author Isaac Asimov, when considering a world where robots had become as functional and intelligent as — and more powerful than — their human creators, posited three fundamental laws that would determine the behavior of such potentially dangerous human-made creations.

His "Three Laws of Robotics" stipulated that non-living human creations must obey humans and never behave in a way that would harm humans.

BEEP
I LOVE YOU!

Aww!

In some famous fictional scenarios, we see the consequences of letting human creations operate without adequate restrictions or limitations.

In Arthur C. Clarke's *2001*, the on-board computer, HAL, seizes control of the spaceship and the humans therein.

The *Terminator* film series depicts a time when human-built machines wage war against humanity itself.

And, in *The Matrix* films, machines use humans much as we now use them.

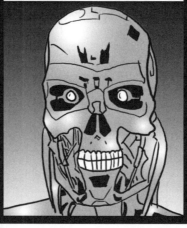

Asimov's idea was profound but not altogether original, of course.

Thomas Jefferson and James Madison beat him to it by about 200 years with the idea that a constitutional amendment was needed to ensure that the reach of corporations was limited.

Something seems to have slipped since then.

SAFE
OBS

It has.

Until 1886, it was a felony in most states for corporations to give money to politicians or otherwise try (through lobbying or advertising) to influence elections.

TAP TAP

Ahem...

Such activity was called "bribery and influencing," and the reason it was banned was simple: corporations can't vote, so what are they doing in politics?

And numerous additional laws were passed to restrain corporations from involvement in politics during the era of President Teddy Roosevelt, who said...

"There can be no effective control of corporations while their political activity remains."

In Wisconsin* for example, the penalty for any corporate official violating the law and getting cozy with politicians on behalf of the corporation was five years in prison and a substantial fine.

But it was only a *little* bribe!

Prior to 1886, corporations were referred to in US law as "artificial persons," similar to the way *Star Trek* portrays the human-looking robot named Data.

Hey bros!

Different family tree.

Seriously.

* The Wisconsin law stated: "No corporation doing business in this state shall pay or contribute, or offer consent or agree to pay or contribute, directly or indirectly, any money, property, free service of its officers or employees or thing of value to any political party, organization, committee or individual for any political purpose whatsoever, or for the purpose of influencing legislation of any kind, or to promote or defeat the candidacy of any person for nomination, appointment or election to any political office."

Like Asimov's Three Laws of Robotics, state laws like that of Wisconsin prevented corporations from harming humans, while still allowing people to create their robots (corporations) and use them to make money.

Everybody won.

But after the Civil War, things began to change.

In the last year of the war, on November 21, 1864, President Abraham Lincoln looked back on the growing power of the war-enriched corporations, and wrote the following thoughtful letter to his friend Colonel William F. Elkins:

*"We may congratulate ourselves that this cruel war is nearing its end ... but I see in the near future **a crisis approaching** that unnerves me and causes me to tremble for the safety of my country.*

*"As a result of the war, **corporations have been enthroned** and an **era of corruption in high places will follow**, and the money power of the country will endeavor to prolong its reign by working upon the prejudices of the people **until all wealth is aggregated in a few hands and the Republic is destroyed.** I feel at this moment more anxiety than ever before, even in the midst of war. God grant that my suspicions may prove groundless."*

Lincoln's suspicions were prescient.

He held the largest corporations — the railroads — at bay until his assassination.

On December 3, 1888, President Grover Cleveland delivered his annual address before a joint session of Congress, two years after the highjacked Santa Clara decision. He said...

"As we view the achievements of aggregated capital, we discover the existence of trusts, combinations, and monopolies, while the citizen is struggling far in the rear or is trampled to death beneath an iron heel. Corporations, which should be the carefully restrained creatures of the law and the servants of the people, are fast becoming the people's masters."

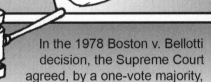

In the 1978 Boston v. Bellotti decision, the Supreme Court agreed, by a one-vote majority, that corporations were "persons"...

...and thus entitled to the free speech right to give huge quantities of money to political causes.

LEGAL

Chief Justice Rehnquist, believing this to be an error, argued that corporations should be restrained from political activity.

In his dissent, Rehnquist implicitly criticized the interpretation of the 1886 Santa Clara case over the years, saying...

"This Court decided at an early date, with neither argument nor discussion, that a business corporation is a 'person' entitled to the protection of the Equal Protection Clause of the Fourteenth Amendment. Santa Clara County v. Southern Pacific R. Co., 118 U.S. 394, 396 (1886)."

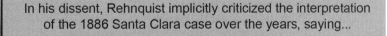

Then he went all the way back to the time of James Monroe's presidency...

...to remind us how the Founders and the Supreme Court's then-Chief Justice John Marshall, a strong Federalist appointed by outgoing President John Adams in 1800, viewed corporations.

Rehnquist wrote:

"Early in our history, Mr. Chief Justice Marshall described the status of a corporation in the eyes of federal law:

'A corporation is an artificial being, invisible, intangible, and existing only in contemplation of law. Being the mere creature of law, it possesses only those properties which the charter of creation confers upon it.'"

Rehnquist concluded his dissent by asserting that it was entirely correct that states have the power to limit a corporation's ability to spend money to influence elections.

I've never heard of corporate "personhood" before. How does it fit in with Bush and the conservative vision?

Let's take a look...

THE DISASTROUS CONSEQUENCES OF CORPORATE "PERSONHOOD"

Corporations have claimed the human rights the Founders fought —

— and sometimes died — to bequeath to living, breathing humans.

And, using those rights, they've usurped our government to the point where our domestic policies are now based on what's best for the corporations with the largest campaign contributions...

...and our foreign policy has become a necessary extension of that.

Before 1886, only humans had full First Amendment rights of free speech, including the right to influence legislation and the right to lie when not under oath.

Now corporations claim that they have the free speech right to influence public opinion and legislation through deceit...

...and have captured control of our airwaves and many of our politicians.

93

Before 1886, only humans had Fourth Amendment rights of privacy.

Since then, however, corporations have claimed that OSHA and EPA* surprise inspections are violations of their human right of privacy, while at the same time asserting their right to perform surprise inspections of their own employees' bodily fluids, phone conversations, and keystrokes.

And they tell us we can't inspect their voting machines that determine the fate of our democracy.

Before 1886, only humans had Fifth Amendment rights against double jeopardy and the right to refuse to speak if they'd committed a crime.

Since 1886, corporations have asserted these human rights for themselves. The results range from today's corporate scandals to 60 years of silence about the deadliness of tobacco and asbestos.

Before 1886, and following the Civil War, only humans had Fourteenth Amendment rights to protection from discrimination.

Since then, corporations have claimed this human right and used it to stop local communities from passing laws to protect their small, local businesses and keep out predatory retailers or large corporations convicted of crimes elsewhere.

*Occupational Safety & Health Administration and Environmental Protection Agency, government agencies charged with protecting health and safety both in and outside the workplace.

As we've seen in a multitude of domestic and international issues, however, our government's policies have been captured by big oil, big auto, and big agriculture — just a few dozen corporations, each richer than the majority of nations on Earth.

Because these corporations have claimed the constitutional human right of free speech (which includes the right to influence legislation, to influence politicians, and give money to political parties) We the People are left out of the decision-making loop.

Hey! What about me!?

And so now, as a handful of the world's largest corporations are working hard and fast to seal the capture of a government that was once the property of We the People, we Americans find ourselves at a crossroads.

From the Bush administration's plan to replace 850,000 government employees with private, unaccountable-to-the-people corporate contractors...

...to the turning of our voting apparatus over to private corporations accountable only to their officers and stockholders...

...to the overwhelming influence large corporations have over our elected representatives through their "free speech" campaign cash...

...we face a stark choice.

Do we want elected representatives making decisions that dramatically affect the quality of our lives and our freedoms...

...or shall we hand these over to private corporations?

FUTURE 1

FUTURE 2

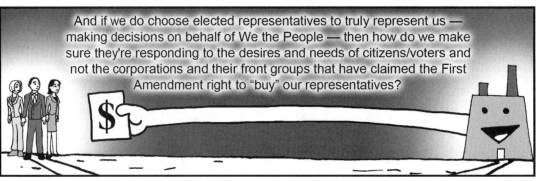

And if we do choose elected representatives to truly represent us — making decisions on behalf of We the People — then how do we make sure they're responding to the desires and needs of citizens/voters and not the corporations and their front groups that have claimed the First Amendment right to "buy" our representatives?

$

RIGHTS

OUT!

PRIVILEGES

Part of the answer must be to return human rights to humans, reversing the theft perpetrated in 1886 by the reporter of the Supreme Court.

Corporations, like government and all other forms of human association, have privileges granted by We the People, but not rights.

Rights are solely the domain of humans.

It's time for America to return to the core value that is embraced by true patriots of every political stripe: that humans have rights, that all other human-created institutions have privileges, and that those privileges are granted, and are therefore revocable, by human voters.

Ending the doctrine of corporate personhood will enable us to restore constitutional democracy to our republic, and restore the power of governance to We the People.

Play nice.

To America's Founders, democracy meant that a government drew its power and legitimacy from its citizens, and must be responsive solely to its citizens, and not to any other institution.

PRIVILEGES

Human Rights are for HUMANS!

It seems to me that being a "citizen" doesn't mean that much anymore.

The return of feudalism has, in effect, made ordinary Americans second-class citizens.

Perhaps the low turnout* in the recent American elections means that the average American has become frustrated or has lost hope.

Clearly the results show what every television advertiser has known for 50 years:

With overwhelming advertising saturation you can sell almost anything to almost anybody.

But when the outcome of a political debate turns on who has the most cash, and the largest sources of that cash are corporations with specific legislative agendas to promote, the democratic election process has become a caricature of itself.

*Hovering around 50% in presidential elections; 10-30% in many local elections.

97

Thus the often-heard response:

Why bother?

A handful of rogue mega-corporations and their "think tank" and "lobbyist" front groups are sullying our democratic waters, corrupting our political processes...

Come in, the water's warm!

Ewwww.... I think I know why.

POLITICAL POOL

...and, through monopolistic behavior, wiping out local businesspeople and putting free enterprise at risk along with the democracy it once nurtured.

COMPETITION

RIGHT-WING TALK RADIO

All Democrats are fat, lazy, and stupid.

...the talk-show host said in grave, serious tones as if he were uttering a sacred truth.

We were driving to Michigan for the holidays, and I was tuning around, listening for the stations I'd worked for two and three decades ago.

I turned the dial.

Another host came on.

It's a Hannity For Humanity house...

No liberals are going to get this house.

...Sean Hannity declared, adding that the Habitat For Humanity home he'd apparently hijacked for his own self-promotion would be given only to a family that swears it's conservative.

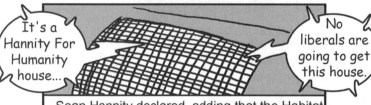

Turning the dial again...

...we found a convicted felon ranting about the importance of government having ever more power to monitor, investigate, and prosecute American citizens without having to worry about constitutional human rights protections.

Apparently the combining of nationwide German police agencies in 1933 into one giant Homeland Security Agency answerable only to the Executive Branch was a lesson of history this guy had completely forgotten.

HOMELAND SECURITY

Police

Border

Neither, apparently, do most Americans recall that the single most powerful device used to bring about the SS and its political master was radio.

In a nation that considers itself a democratic republic, the institutions of democracy are imperiled by a lack of balanced national debate on issues of critical importance.

As both Nazi Germany and Stalinist Russia learned, a steady drumbeat of a single viewpoint — from either end of the political spectrum — is not healthy for democracy when opposing voices are marginalized.

So, is history repeating itself?

Let's see what you think.

Setting aside the shrill and nonsensical efforts of those who suggest that the corporate-owned media in America is "liberal," the situation with regard to talk radio is particularly perplexing:

It doesn't even carry a pretense of political balance.

...those who listen to talk radio know it has swung so far to the right that even Dwight Eisenhower or Barry Goldwater would be shocked.

Did he just say what I thought he said?!

While the often-understated Al Gore recently came right out and said that much of the corporate-owned media are...

"part and parcel of the Republican Party"...

Average Americans across the nation are wondering how could it be that a small fringe of the extreme right has so captured the nation's airwaves?

And done it in such an effective fashion that when they attack folks like Senate Minority Leader Tom Daschle, he and his family actually get increased numbers of death threats?

Vote Conservative.

Vote Conservative.

How is it that ex-felons like John Poindexter's Iran-Contra protégé Ollie North and Nixon's former burglar G. Gordon Liddy have become stars?

How is it that ideologues like Rush Limbaugh can openly promote hard-right Republicans...

Vote Conservative.

...and avoid a return of the dead-since-Reagan Fairness Doctrine...

LEFT   RIGHT

...and dodge the political-activity provisions of the McCain/Feingold campaign finance reform bill (getting around the desire of the American public for fairness)...

...by claiming what they do is:

"just entertainment"?

Vote Conservative.

And, given the domination of talk radio by the fringe hard-right that represents the political views of only a small segment of America, why is it that the vast majority of talk radio stations across the nation never run even an occasional centrist or progressive show in the midst of their all-right, all-the-time programming day?

There's gotta be something!?

It is increasingly obvious that big media companies have been committed to exclusively promoting the most hard-right elements of the Republican Party.

The MSNBC cable television network dumped liberal talk-media pioneer Phil Donahue even though his was the most highly rated show on the network.

Hard-right radio talker Glen Beck organized pro-war/pro-Bush events all across the nation.

I SUPPORT BUSH AND OUR TROOPS (and senseless death)

FREE IRAQ

Radio stations ran highly publicized Dixie Chicks censorships and CD-burnings after one of the Chicks admitted embarrassment at being from the same state as the president.

Down with the Dixie Chicks!

EVIDENCE OF FREE SPEECH

And both Limbaugh and Hannity went into Republican hyperdrive with born-again Bush-can-do-no-wrong riffs...

Master!

...that defied traditional conservative values by embracing the bizarre idea that somehow deficits are good...

BIZARRO MATH

$$ \$ + \downarrow = \text{Success} $$

...taxpayer-funded photo-ops are wonderful...

...and insider politicians profiting from their knowledge and access are no longer worth mentioning.

(All things Clinton was savaged and/or investigated for.)

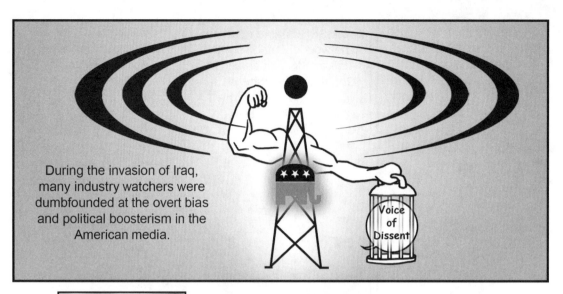

During the invasion of Iraq, many industry watchers were dumbfounded at the overt bias and political boosterism in the American media.

Even BBC Director General Greg Dyke weighed in, saying...

"I was shocked while in the United States by how unquestioning the broadcast news media was during this war."

Across America and around the world, savvy media watchers wondered out loud why our giant networks and media companies would suddenly become so overtly partisan...

...loudly and unquestioningly kissing up to the Bush administration?

And why did they ignore a multi-million-dollar audience of tens of millions of Democratic/liberal listeners — people with upscale demographics that advertisers would love to reach?

Hey! I'm an audience too!

THOUGHT CONTROL IN AMERICA

Right-wing talk radio is only the most obvious slice of what appears to many Americans to be a biased and highly controlled media system that supports an administration running wild.

But, just as recognition of the relationship between Big Oil and the Bush family makes the Iraq War appear to be "logical"...

...corporate control of government *requires* corporate control of information.

In a speech recorded in the 1992 documentary film, *Manufacturing Consent*, cultural observer, linguist and political activist **Noam Chomsky** zeroed in on the reasons for and the mechanisms of corporate media's exercise of what he calls "thought control in a democratic society."

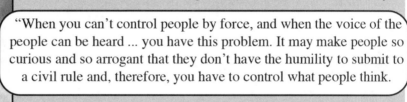

"When you can't control people by force, and when the voice of the people can be heard ... you have this problem. It may make people so curious and so arrogant that they don't have the humility to submit to a civil rule and, therefore, you have to control what people think.

"The standard way to do this ... is to resort to what, in more honest days, used to be called propaganda: manufacture of consent, creation of necessary illusions, various ways of either marginalizing the general public or reducing them to apathy in some fashion."

How do the corporate media serve the interests of the corporations and politicians that dominate our society?

Chomsky says that the process starts with the selection (and rejection) of topics to cover.

✓ "Terrorism"   ~~Globalization Negatives~~
~~Privatization~~   ~~Loss of the Commons~~
✓ Consumer Business Market   ~~Corporate Personhood~~
~~Public Manipulation~~   ✓ Taxes
~~Corporate Welfare~~   ~~Government Corruption~~
~~Corporate Corruption~~   ~~Vote Theft~~

The media then restrictively frame issues, add emphasis and filter out information that might not support their position.

And, most importantly, they set the boundaries of the debate.

ROUND 1
CONSERVATIVE
versus
MODERATE CONSERVATIVE

"The problem has gotten so severe," ...write Robert W. McChesney and John Nichols in *Our Media Not Theirs* "that the media system has become a major barrier to the exercise of democracy and to the discussion of any of the mounting social problems that face us."

CORPORATIONS CLAIM THE RIGHT TO LIE

While sports product giant Nike was conducting a huge and expensive public relations blitz to tell people that it had cleaned up its subcontractors' sweatshop labor practices...

...an alert consumer advocate and activist in California named Marc Kasky caught them in what he alleged were a number of specific deceptions.

Citing a California law that forbids corporations from intentionally deceiving people in their commercial statements, Kasky sued the multi-billion-dollar corporation.

Instead of refuting Kasky's charge by proving in court that they did not lie, Nike chose to argue that corporations should enjoy the same "free speech" right to deceive that individual human citizens have in their personal lives.

If people have the constitutionally protected right to say...

..."The check's in the mail."

...or...

"That looks great on you."

...then (Nike's reasoning goes) a corporation should have the same right to say whatever they want in their corporate PR campaigns.

I ♥ you, babes!

They took this argument all the way to the California Supreme Court, where they lost.

Ha! Score one for humans!

The California court decided that Nike was engaging in commercial speech, which the state can regulate under truth-in-advertising and other laws.

Persistent, Nike appealed to the U.S. Supreme Court early in 2003, claiming that, as a "person," this multinational corporation has a constitutional free-speech right to deceive.

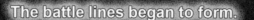

The battle lines began to form.

Corporate America rose up, and — unlike you and me — when large corporations "speak" they can use a billion-dollar bullhorn.

The U.S. Chamber of Commerce, Exxon/Mobil, Monsanto, Microsoft, Pfizer, and Bank of America filed "friend of the court" briefs supporting Nike.

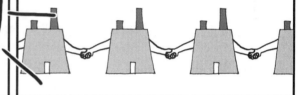

Additionally,

virtually all

of the nation's largest corporate-owned news-papers editorialized in favor of Nike and gave virtually no coverage to or even printed letters to the editor asserting the humans' side of the case.

On the side of "only humans have human rights" was the lone human activist in California, Marc Kasky, who brought the original complaint against Nike.

Woefully, not even the ACLU weighed in on his side, although some public interest groups — including Global Exchange, Public Citizen, ReclaimDemocracy.org, and Sierra Club — filed their own amicus briefs on his behalf.

This is SO wrong!

In a column in the New York Times supporting Nike's position, Bob Herbert wrote...

"In a real democracy, even the people you disagree with get to have their say."

True enough, but Nike isn't a person —

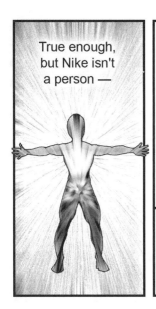

— it's a corporation.

And it's not their "say" they're asking for: it's the right to deceive people.

Unfortunately, the U.S. Supreme Court declined to hear Nike's appeal of the California Supreme Court's decision.

I say "unfortunately" because I believe that the Chief Justice of the Court might have sided with humans...

...proving that this is an issue that is neither conservative nor progressive, but rather one that has to do with

democracy versus corporate plutocracy.

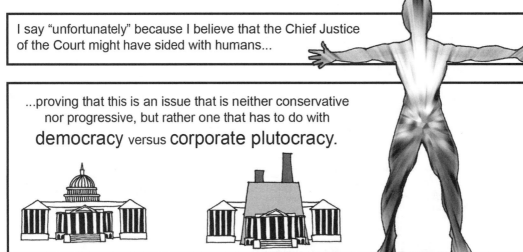

If the Court had chosen to hear the Kasky v. Nike case, it could have opened an opportunity for them to rule that corporations don't have the free speech right to knowingly deceive the public.

It's even possible that the Court might have revisited the error of Davis's 1886 headnote...

...and begun the process of dismantling the flawed and unconstitutional doctrine of corporate personhood.

With this lost opportunity to turn back the clock on the corporate takeover of public opinion, We the People will have to wait for another day and another venue to bring big corporations back inside the rule of law.

This is just so weird. It's like we're all part of some fantasy, some movie, like *1984*...

I know...

...and in this adventure we each get to cast ourselves in the hero or heroine's role.

Our individual and collective choices —

— every action we take or don't —

— will determine the outcome of the story.

THE THEFT OF YOUR VOTE

In the earliest democracy, there was no voting.

THOM HARTMANN
author

The Athenian Greeks had an annual lottery, and every citizen was in the pool.

When your name was drawn, you had to serve in the Polis, or legislature, for a year.

THOMIUS HARTMANNIUS

At the end of the year, you were replaced by a new person selected in the lottery.

TOGA PARTY IN THE POLIS!

Sort of like jury duty.

What made democracy unique, in the mind of its inventors, wasn't voting.

That was just a means to the end.

What's unique about democracy is that it's the only form of governance in the 6,000 year history of modern civilization in which the power, authority, and credibility of government is derived from its citizens, and from its citizens alone.

Whether by lottery or by voting, it is the citizens who both comprise and direct the government.

...and the people could thus examine their processes and results.

Even Goldwater, ever suspicious of the creeping power of government, approved.

The process was relatively transparent.

FAIR AND ACCURATE

But since the 2000 elections, things have changed radically.

It turns out that the computer-controlled, modem-connected voting machines hastily rushed into many states in the wake of the 2000 election irregularities...

...are the property of, and operated by, private corporations.

And some of those corporations have apparently told We the People that we have no right to inspect their machines' innards, no freedom to audit their processes...

No peeking!

Hey!

...and no ability to determine why their results are so dramatically at variance with our exit polls...

Hmmm...

2 voters + 3 voters 6 votes?

Exit Polls

...that in 2002 our polling companies had to sit down, shut up, and scratch their heads in bewilderment.

POLLSTERS

WHY!?

I know I can count!

This private, corporate takeover of the voting process at the very core of democracy raises disturbing issues about who controls the fate and future of our nation.

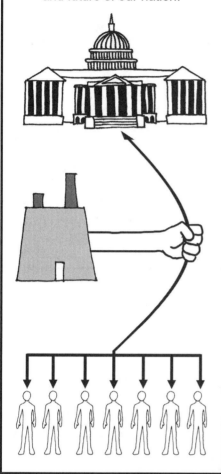

We may still have a chance to continue America's noble experiment with democratic government, but only if we understand the history of computer voting and change course quickly.

1976
1984
1992
2000
2002
2004

Wait a minute! Just how serious do you think this is?

This could just be the biggest story in America right now.

Because you contend that computerized voting machines offer a wide-open back door to massive voting fraud?

It's not just me. The discussion has moved from the Internet to CNN, to UK newspapers, and the pages of *The New York Times*.

People are beginning to connect the dots, and the picture that's emerging is troubling.

November 7, 2002

SNYDER, Texas (AP) — A defective computer chip in the county's optical scanner misread ballots Tuesday night and incorrectly tallied a landslide victory for Republicans. Democrats actually won by wide margins.

Republicans would have carried the day had not poll workers become suspicious when the computerized vote-reading machines said the Republican candidate was trouncing his incumbent Democratic opponent in the race for County Commissioner.

A quick hand recount of the optical-scan ballots showed that the Democrat had indeed won.

OUT   IN

When a new chip was later installed, the computer verified the Democratic victory.

In another Texas anomaly, three Comal County candidates received identical vote counts:

House of Representatives

Republican Carter Casteel won her state house seat with exactly 18,181 votes.

 **State Senate**

Republican State Senator Jeff Wentworth won his race with exactly 18,181 votes.

 18,181

Conservative Judge Danny Scheel won his seat with exactly 18,181 votes.

Apparently, however, no poll workers in Comal County thought to ask for a new chip.*

The Texas incidents happened with computerized machines reading and then tabulating paper or punch-card ballots.

In Georgia and Florida, where paper had been totally replaced by touch-screen machines in many to most precincts during 2001 and 2002, the 2002 election produced some of the nation's most startling results.

*www.co.comal.tx.us/Election_Results2002.htm

Atlanta Journal-Constitution

November 2, 2002

ATLANTA — *Journal-Constitution* poll shows Democratic Sen. Max Cleland with a 49%-to-44% lead over Republican Rep. Saxby Chambliss.

November 7, 2002

Cox News Service

ATLANTA — Republican Rep. Saxby Chambliss defeated incumbent Democratic Sen. Max Cleland by a margin of 53 to 46 percent. … The Hotline, a political news service, recalled a series of polls Wednesday showing that Chambliss had been ahead in none of them.

Just as amazing was the Georgia governor's race.

Republican Sonny Perdue won over incumbent Democratic Gov. Roy Barnes by a margin of 52 to 45 percent.

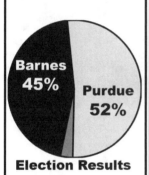

Barnes 45% **Purdue 52%**

Election Results

The most recent Mason Dixon Poll had shown Barnes ahead 48 to 39 percent the previous month with a margin of error of plus or minus 4 points.

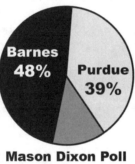

Barnes 48% **Purdue 39%**

Mason Dixon Poll

www.zogby.com/soundbites/ReadClips.dbm?ID=4864

Almost all of the votes in Georgia were recorded on the new touch screen computerized voting machines, which produced no paper trail whatsoever.

San Jose Mercury News

January 23, 2003

Gee Whiz, Voter Fraud?

In one Florida precinct last November, votes that were intended for the Democratic candidate for governor ended up for Gov. Jeb Bush, because of a misaligned touch screen.

How many votes were miscast before the mistake was found will never be known, because there was no paper audit.*

Apparently, nobody thought to ask for new chips in Florida, either.

Meanwhile, Minnesota Sen. Paul Wellstone's sudden death set up another odd result…

*www.bayarea.com/mld/mercurynews/news/opinion/5011944.htm

113

Minnesota Star Tribune

October 30, 2002

Wellstone's likely replacement on the ballot, former Vice President Walter Mondale, leads Republican Norm Coleman by 47 to 39 percent — close to where the race stood two weeks ago when Wellstone led Coleman 47 to 41 percent.

When the computerized machines were done counting the vote a few days later, however, Coleman had beaten Mondale by 50 to 47 percent.

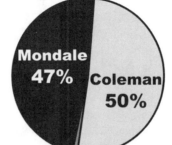

Mondale 47%
Coleman 50%

If Mondale had asked for new chips, would it have made a difference?

We'll never know.

With no verification method — no paper trails — all of our computerized voting will therefore be suspect?

Right. It's naïve to think that humans will stop trying to manipulate or cheat in elections any time soon.

Therefore, the priorities have to remain focused —

on fairness

accuracy

...and, most of all...

accountability.

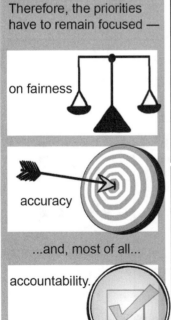

And as long as corporations refuse to let us know what's going on inside the machines...

...it's crucial that government should own and operate the mechanism of voting that is at the heart of democracy.

What I'm telling you is just the tip of the iceberg of '00, '02 and '04 election irregularities, as reported by www.votewatch.us.

Either the system by which democracy exists broke those November evenings...

...or was hacked...

...or American voters became suddenly more fickle than at any time since Truman beat Dewey.

Maybe it's true that the citizens of Georgia simply decided that incumbent Democratic Senator Max Cleland, a wildly popular war veteran...

....was, as Republican TV ads suggested, too unpatriotic to remain in the Senate...

...even though his Republican challenger, Saxby Chambliss, had sat out the Vietnam War with student and medical deferments.

Student Deferment

Medical Deferment

Maybe, in the final two days of the race, those voters who'd pledged themselves to Georgia's popular incumbent Governor Roy Barnes...

...suddenly and inexplicably decided to switch to Republican challenger Sonny Perdue.

I ♥ Barnes!

NO! I ♥ Perdue!

Maybe, Alabama's new Republican governor Bob Riley, and a small but congressionally decisive handful of long-shot Republican candidates around the country really did win those states...

...where conventional wisdom and straw polls showed them losing in the last few election cycles,...

...but computer controlled voting or ballot-reading machines showed them winning.

Perhaps, after a half-century of fine-tuning exit polling to such a science that it's now used to verify if elections are clean in Third World countries...

Looks good!

EXIT POLLS

"THIRD WORLD" →

...it really did suddenly become inaccurate in the United States in the past few years and just won't work here anymore.

Broken!

Perhaps it's just a coincidence that the sudden rise of inaccurate exit polls happened around the same time corporate-programmed, computer-controlled, modem-capable voting machines began recording and tabulating ballots.

But if any of this is true, there's not much of a paper trail from the voters' hands to prove it.

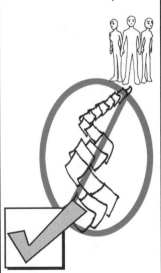

You'd think in an open democracy that the government — answerable to all its citizens...

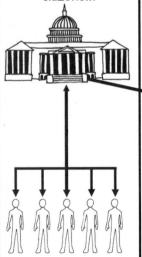

...rather than a handful of corporate officers and stockholders —

— would program, repair and control the voting machines.

You'd think the computers that handle our cherished ballots would be open and their software and programming available for public scrutiny.

You'd think there would be a paper trail of the actual hand-cast vote...

...which could be followed and audited if there was evidence of voting fraud or if exit polls disagreed with computerized vote counts...

But?

You'd be wrong.

How widespread does this seem to be?

Good question. Let's look at another state.

It's entirely possible that Nebraska Republican Chuck Hagel —

— who left his job as head of an electronic voting machine company to run as a long-shot candidate for the U.S. Senate —

— legitimately won all of his elections.

Back when Hagel first ran for the U.S. Senate in 1996, his own company's computer-controlled voting machines showed he'd won **stunning and unexpected victories** in both the primaries and the general election.

HAGEL

According to Bev Harris of www.blackboxvoting.org, Hagel won virtually every demographic group, including many largely black communities that **had never before voted Republican.**

Anything's possible... right?

Hagel was the first Republican in 24 years to win a Senate seat in Nebraska.

Six years later Hagel ran again, this time against Democrat Charlie Matulka in 2002, and won in a landslide.

Mount Election

About 80 percent of those votes were counted by computer-controlled voting machines put in place by the company affiliated with Hagel:

80%
HAGEL

Built by that company.

Programmed by that company.

01011101

Containing chips supplied by that company.

"This is a big story, bigger than Watergate ever was"

said Matulka*

Is Matulka the just a sore loser as the Hagel campaign paints him...

...or is he democracy's proverbial canary in the mineshaft?

Between them, Hagel and Chambliss' victories sealed Republican control of the Senate.

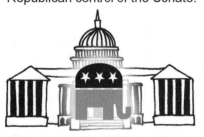

Chances are both won fair and square, the American way:

...using huge piles of corporate money to carpet-bomb voters with television advertising.

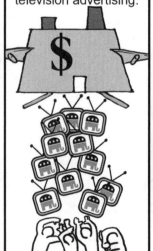

But either the appearance or the possibility of impropriety in an election casts a shadow over American democracy.

In your book, you include something Thomas Paine wrote over 200 years ago...

"The right of voting for representatives is the primary right by which all other rights are protected. To take away this right is to reduce a man to slavery."

That slavery may be at our doorstep.

THOM HARTMANN
author

As Charlie Matulka suggests, "They can take over our country without firing a shot, just by taking over our election systems."

Even with all you've described, is that really possible?

Increasing numbers of people think so.

Bev Harris has studied the situation in depth and thinks Matulka and other observers may be on to something.

The company with ties to Hagel even threatened her with legal action when she went public about the company having built the machines that counted Hagel's landslide votes.

Keep yer mouth shut!

In the meantime, exit-polling organizations have quietly gone out of business, replaced by media consortiums whose exit polls still vary from "official" results — but only in some states...

LSTERS

CLOSED

...and the news arms of the huge multinational corporations that own our TV networks are suggesting the days of exit polls are over...

...and in 2004 former Enron lobbyist and RNC chairman Ed Gillespie suggested they be ended altogether in the U.S.

Virtually none were reported in 2002, creating an odd and unsettling silence that caused unease for the many voters who had come to view exit polls as proof of the integrity of their election systems. When tried again in 2004, inconsistencies still flourished.

As all this comes to light, many citizens and even a few politicians are wondering if it's a good idea for corporations to be so involved in the guts of our voting systems.

The whole idea of a democratic republic was to create a common institution — the government itself— owned by its citizens, answerable to its citizens and authorized to exist and continue existing solely "by the consent of the governed."

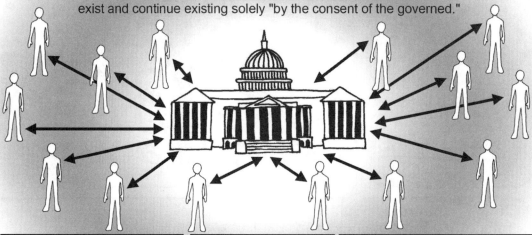

However, the recent political trend has moved us in the opposite direction, with governments turning administration of our Commons over to corporations answerable only to profits.

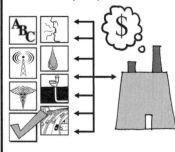

As a result: corporations are being enriched...

...and America is starting to resemble a banana republic.

Further frustrating those concerned with the sanctity of our vote, the corporations selling and licensing voting machines and voting software often claim Fourth Amendment rights of privacy and the right to hide their "trade secrets"...

— how their voting software works and what controls are built into it —

— from both the public and the government itself.

What's happening to the votes?!

"If you want to make Coca-Cola and have trade secrets, that's fine"...

...says Harvard's Rebecca Mercuri, Ph.D., one of the nation's leading experts on voting machines.

"But don't try to claim trade secrets when you're handling our votes."

Who owns whom among the various companies is often under wraps, too, as most of them are not publicly traded companies.

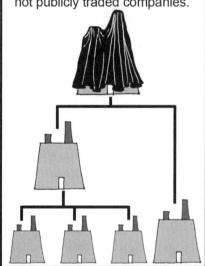

One voting machine company was partially funded at startup by wealthy Republican philanthropists who belong to an organization that believes the Bible instead of the Constitution should govern America.

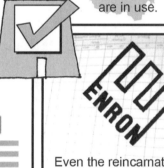

The head of another said he was "committed to helping Ohio deliver its electoral votes to the president," a state where their machines are in use.

Even the reincarnation of a company that helped Enron cook their books has gotten into the act.

"There are several issues here"...

...says reporter Lynn Landes, who has written extensively about voting machines.

"First, there's the issue that the Voting Rights Act requires that poll watchers be able to observe the vote. But with computerized voting machines, your vote vanishes into a computer and can't be observed."

To solve this, many are calling for a return to paper ballots that are hand-counted.

It may be slower, but temp-help precinct workers may even cost less than electronic voting machines (which represent a multi-billion-dollar boon for corporate suppliers)...

...and will ensure that real humans are tabulating the vote.

"Second," says Landes,

"there's the issue of who controls the information. Of all the functions of government that should not be privatized, handling our votes is at the top of the list. This is the core of democracy, and must be open, transparent, and available to both the public and our politicians of all parties for full and open inspection."

Most government functions — from our courts to our fire departments — run fairly smoothly, despite carping from the extreme right wing.

ARRGH! IT'S NOT PERFECT!

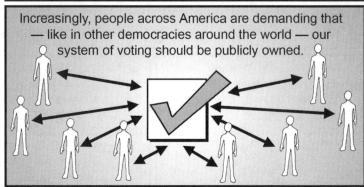

Increasingly, people across America are demanding that — like in other democracies around the world — our system of voting should be publicly owned.

Another issue that Dr. Mercuri raises is the Help America Vote Act (HAVA) — passed after problems arose in the 2002 election primaries.

Says Mercuri,

"Sadly, HAVA turned out to be just another example of pork-barrel politics. The Federal government allocated $3 billion to be used by States that wanted to update their election equipment. But HAVA's voting system standards will not be available until 2006, after all of the equipment purchases are required to have been made, so all of the new equipment is guaranteed to be obsolete."

"As well, voting system standards lack the computer security controls commonly applied in the defense, banking, aviation and healthcare industries. Even casino gaming and lottery ticket machines are more securely designed than ballot casting and counting devices."

So, who does this delay, this ensured obsolescence, benefit?

C'mon baby, poppa needs a brand new president!

Sure enough, the 2004 elections produced an array of dubious voting results. In Broward County Florida, a computer subtracted 70,000 votes because it started counting in reverse after hitting a software "ceiling".

Another in North Carolina lost more than 4,500 votes because it couldn't store enough data.

Meanwhile, a voting machine in Franklin County Ohio gave George W. Bush 3,893 extra votes in a district where only 638 total votes were cast.

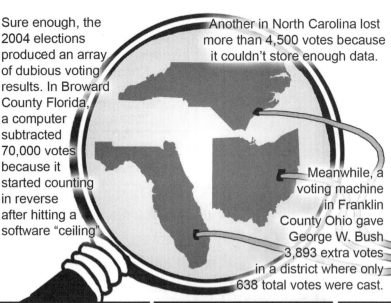

While corporate bungles or the potential for outright vote fraud are a concern of many opposed to electronic voting machines...

...another issue of concern is the concentration of voter rolls in the hands of partisan politicians instead of civil servants.

In most states, local precincts or counties maintain their own voter rolls.

Florida, however, had gone to the trouble before the 2000 election to consolidate all its voter rolls at the state level...

...and put them into the custody and control of the state's elected Secretary of State, Katherine Harris, who was also the chairman of the Florida campaign to elect George W. Bush.

As described in disturbing detail in the documentary *Unprecedented* and in Greg Palast's book *The Best Democracy Money Can Buy*, Harris paid DBT, a Texas company, $4.3 million to "clean up" the Florida voter list by purging it of all convicted felons...

...using a list of tens of millions of ex-felons in the U.S.

One of the legacies of slavery is that a large number of African Americans share the same or similar names...

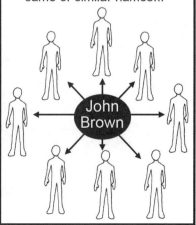

...and sure enough, when the DBT felon list was compared with the Florida voter list over 94,000 matches or near-matches were found.

Those registered Florida voters — about half of them African Americans (who generally vote Democratic) —

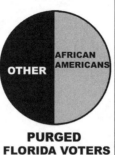

OTHER AFRICAN AMERICANS

PURGED FLORIDA VOTERS

— with names identical or merely similar to those of ex-felons were deleted from the Florida voter rolls, and turned away from the polls when they tried to vote in 2000 and in 2002.

Charles William   Kira Klatchko

John Pacheco   Ken Zeiglar

Amy Flores   James Ehrlich

Vineet Kumar   Erik Beckman

Joe Ali   Michael Segal

John Engstrom   Jared Coates

Theodore Mason   Ken Faiman

Christina Obligar   John Brown

Ben Hartshorne   Chris Vrabel

The irony of the Florida purge is that, in some cases, scores of voters with the same name were prevented from voting.

John Brown John Brown
John Brown John Brown
John Brown John Brown
John Brown John Brown
John Brown John Brown
John Brown John Brown
John Brown John Brown
John Brown John Brown

And apparently neither DBT nor the Florida Secretary of State attempted to confirm that a single voter purged from election rolls was actually an ex-felon.

John Brown

Now, under HAVA, states across the nation are consolidating their voter lists and handing them over to Harris's various peers to be cleaned and maintained.

This is beginning to sound very scary.

Yeah, and that's not all.

Another concern is Internet voting, since it's impossible to ensure its accuracy.

Imagine if all the time a voting machine was being used, it also had its back door open and an unlimited number of technicians and hackers could manipulate its innards before, during and after the vote.

Hey! Who are you guys?!

Oh... don't mind me!

Activists suggest that the danger lies in the fact that so many electronic voting machines today are connected to company-access modems.

Personally, I think it's scandalous to even consider handling our vote — the very core of democracy — in uncontrollable and insecure cyberspace.

Nonetheless, the Pentagon has considered plans to have a private corporation conduct Internet voting for overseas GIs in 2004...

...and many fear that it will be used as a beta test for more widespread Internet voting across the nation.

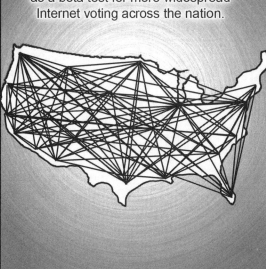

While many Americans think the ability to vote from home or office over the computer would be wonderfully convenient, the results could be disastrous.

It's so easy!

Even the hyper-security-conscious CIA hasn't been able to prevent hackers from penetrating parts of its computer systems attached to the Internet.

What I hear you saying is that, in America, the people may no longer "own" the government.

Ownership implies control, and control is rapidly being lost.

On most levels, privatization is only a "small sin" against democracy.

Don't worry, I'm okay without them.

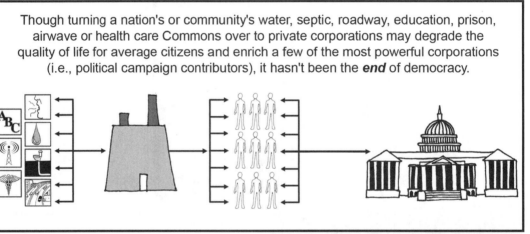

Though turning a nation's or community's water, septic, roadway, education, prison, airwave or health care Commons over to private corporations may degrade the quality of life for average citizens and enrich a few of the most powerful corporations (i.e., political campaign contributors), it hasn't been the **end** of democracy.

Many citizens believe, however, that turning the programming and maintenance of voting over to corporations that can share their profits openly with politicians (or, like Hagel, become the politicians)...

...puts democracy itself in peril.

Growing numbers of Americans are saying that our votes are too sacred to reside only on "chips"...

...that it's critical that we kick corporations out of the Commons of our voting...

...and that we make sure we have a human-verifiable vote paper trail that goes all the way back to the original hand of the original voter.

If there are chips involved in the voting process, these democracy advocates say, government civil service employees who are subject to adversarial oversight by all major parties must program them in an open-source fashion, and in a way that produces a voter-verified paper trail.

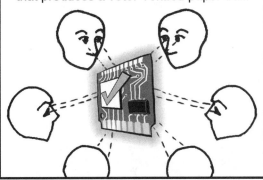

Anything less, and it could be the last nail in the coffin of American democracy.

My God, can't you leave us with anything positive?

Sure. We need to act quickly and decisively to avoid catastrophe, but there's plenty we can do to turn the tide.

TURNING THE TIDE

To every Middlesex village and farm,
A cry of defiance, and not of fear,
A voice in the darkness,
 a knock at the door,
And a word that shall echo for evermore!
For, borne on the night-wind of the Past,
Through all our history, to the last,
In the hour of darkness
 and peril and need,
The people will waken
 and listen to hear.

— From *Paul Revere's Ride*
by *Henry Wadsworth Longfellow, 1863*

Only a public revolt in disgust over the unconscionable behavior of today's conservatives will stop them from turning America into a corporate-based clone of Mussolini's feudal vision.

It is again that hour —

— "the hour of darkness and peril and need" —

— and now is the time for We the Rabble to re-awaken our fellow citizens.

Thankfully, there's a growing movement all across America to rescue democracy from extinction at the conservatives' hands.

Communities have passed resolutions and laws denying corporate personhood...

...and cases that could bring these questions into the open — like Kasky v. Nike — are showing up before the Supreme Court.

Perhaps most importantly, the naked corporate grab of government in an administration made almost entirely of corporate CEOs is being exposed almost every day.

Eep!

Following the Women's Suffrage Movement of the late 19th and early 20th centuries...

VOTES FOR WOMEN

...and the Women's Rights Movement of the 1970s...

WOMEN'S RIGHTS NOW!

EQUAL RIGHTS EQUAL [PAY!]

...a third wave of women's influence in politics seems to be emerging — perhaps best exemplified by the Code Pink organization's serious yet playful grassroots activities.

MOTHERS OPPOSE

PEACE

They add great flair and visibility to their political demonstrations and vigils by the simple tactic of asking participants to dress in pink. (www.codepinkalert.org)

A network of women elders, the Raging Grannies, also uses humor, song and street theater effectively to raise public awareness about peace, justice, and equality.

Time for some reform, kids!

(www.raginggrannies.com)

Organizations and websites offering perspectives on participatory or deliberative democracy — things like citizen or consensus councils — have been springing up like mushrooms.

CIVIL RIGHTS

CORPORATE CRIMES

ELECTION FRAUD

ANTI-WAR

Activist Tom Atlee's website (www.democracyinnovations.org) lists over a hundred such innovations.

Thanks to Internet radio and new technological ventures like Sirius Satellite Radio, liberal/progressive talk radio is an emerging reality — often running 24 hours of programming daily.

Radio stations across the nation are starting to seek out progressive programming. My own program, which broadcasts at the same time as Rush Limbaugh, is being picked up by new stations at a steady pace.

Unions, the traditional defenders of working-class people, are becoming more politically active and pointing out that all people who draw a paycheck —

— be they blue- or white-collar workers — are suffering from the new American feudalism.

Check out www.uaw.org and www.aflcio.org for insight into how sophisticated America's unions are in their understanding of the conservative agenda, and how it can be challenged.

Hopefully, one day soon such open plain speaking may even reach the website of the party founded by Thomas Jefferson...

...although for now the activist-run www.democrats.com site far outstrips the Party's www.democrats.org for clarity, purpose, and political momentum.

Perhaps, as Leonard Cohen sings,

"Democracy is coming to the U.S.A."

If so, while the opportunity is still available to us, this nation's citizens must listen, join, share, read, campaign, and enlighten themselves and others, in order to roll back the damage done by the "conservative feudalists."

If we are to bring democracy back to the land of its modern rebirth we must

awaken

step forth

and speak out.

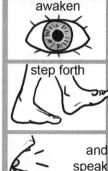

The pen is mightier than the sword, we're told...

...and the power of the **word** in the hands of ordinary citizens is even greater today than it was at the time of the first American Revolution thanks to:

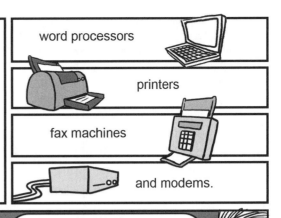

word processors

printers

fax machines

and modems.

In 1773, the Founders of our nation faced off against the East India Company's corporate feudalism.

Their voices unheard in the halls of the British government or even in many of the newspapers of the day, they turned to two very effective, nonviolent methods to spread the new concept of democracy.

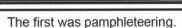

The first was pamphleteering.

The Internet is today's pamphlet. Millions are using e-mail and directing others to websites that offer to awaken people and promote democratic change.

The second method involved the creation of "committees of correspondence," also used extensively by the Women's Suffrage movement a century later. These were groups organized to write letters to the editors of newspapers.

Today, people across America have already begun letter writing, faxing, and e-mail campaigns, and one sees the results on the editorial pages of our newspapers and in the reactions of some of our politicians.

Other correspondents are blogging* or calling in to talk shows, modern variations on this theme.

It's quite important for those who want to turn the tide, to call their local stations (both talk and music) to let them know that they want to hear progressive or Democratic voices, and that they will patronize the advertisers of such shows .

*Creating a running commentary online; "blog" is short for "web log."

THE THIRD AMERICAN REVOLUTION

Thomas Jefferson wrote the Declaration of Independence, which explicitly stated that humans were born into this world endowed by their Creator with certain rights...

...that governments were created by humans to insure that only humans held those rights...

...and that...

"whenever any form of government becomes destructive of these ends, it is the right of the people to alter or abolish it."

Stating flatly that

"it is their right, it is their duty,"

to alter their government and thus claim their unique human rights...

...56 men defied the East India Company and the government whose army supported it by placing their signatures on the Declaration of Independence, saying,

"with a firm reliance on the protection of divine Providence, we mutually pledge to each other our Lives, our Fortunes and our sacred Honor."

Thus began America's first experiment with democracy.

In December 1776, Thomas Paine published a pamphlet that declared...

"Tyranny, like hell, is not easily conquered. ... What we obtain too cheap, we esteem too lightly: it is dearness only that gives every thing its value. Heaven knows how to put a proper price upon its goods; and it would be strange indeed if so celestial an article as **freedom** should not be highly rated."

The little-known Second American Revolution involved the dethroning of the second president, John Adams, who had a lot more in common with George W. Bush than one might suspect.

But more on that later.

This brings us up to the present and the Third Revolution, which, in fact, has a lot in common with the First...

As you recall, in 1773 the East India Company claimed the "right" to participate in the political processes of England and, with wealth and power far greater than the average citizen, got passed for themselves a huge tax reduction on tea...

...and an overall tax rebate so large that they could undersell and wipe out their small Colonial competitors.

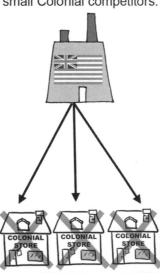

The response of the entrepreneurial colonists to the Tea Act of 1773 was the Boston Tea Party revolt against that transnational corporation...

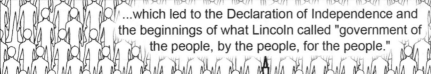

...which led to the Declaration of Independence and the beginnings of what Lincoln called "government of the people, by the people, for the people."

The Third Revolution was set in motion in 2000 when one of the largest sludge-hauling corporations in the United States sued Porter Township, PA, over the municipality's adoption of a per-ton fee for dumping Pittsburgh-generated sludge in the area.

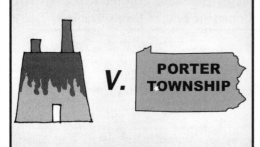

V. PORTER TOWNSHIP

The sludge company claimed that as a "person" it had rights equal to the citizens of the township...

...and, therefore, the township couldn't "discriminate" against the corporation under the due process and equal protection clauses of the 14th Amendment, which was passed after the Civil War to free the slaves.

Ha!

Supported by a powerful coalition of pro-democracy groups, Porter Township fought back.*

They bluntly asserted that — as it was from the founding of this nation until the bizarre Santa Clara County v. Southern Pacific Railroad Supreme Court case in 1886...

— only humans are entitled to human rights in their community.

The democratically elected municipal officials of Porter Township put their signatures to an ordinance passed unanimously on December 9, 2002.

It declares that corporations are legal fictions and that interpreting the Constitution to consider them as persons has ...

"long wrought havoc with our democratic processes."

It further states that such misconstrued rights combined with corporate wealth were usurping the constitutional rights of their township's citizens.

Hey!

And then, with an audacity like that displayed by the Founders, the elders of Porter Township said...

"Democracy means government by the people. … Corporations shall not be considered to be 'persons' protected by the Constitution of the United States or the Constitution of the Commonwealth of Pennsylvania."

It became the law of that land five days later.**

* That coalition included the Pennsylvania Farmers Union, the Pennsylvania Association for Sustainable Agriculture, The Sierra Club, the AFL-CIO, the United Mine Workers of America, Common Cause, the Program on Corporations, Law, and Democracy (POCLAD), and the Community Environmental Legal Defense Fund (CELDF).
** See Appendix B for more about undoing corporate personhood.

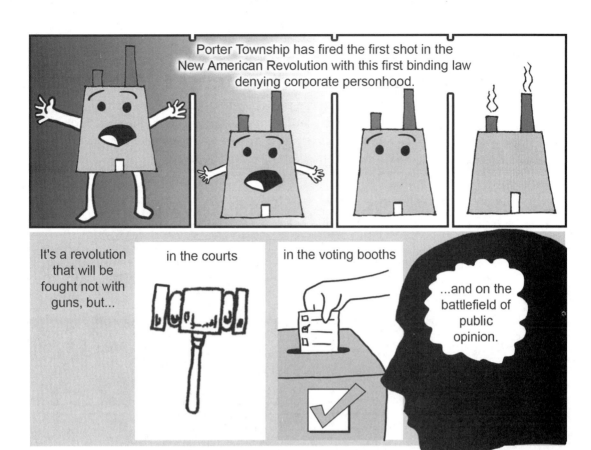

Porter Township has fired the first shot in the New American Revolution with this first binding law denying corporate personhood.

It's a revolution that will be fought not with guns, but...

in the courts

in the voting booths

...and on the battlefield of public opinion.

And, far from harming American business, returning human rights solely to humans will lead to an entrepreneurial renaissance.

Only a handful of very large corporations use or abuse these "rights" in order to deceive people, hide crimes, or make politicians violate the will of their own voters.

Stop making us all look bad!

The millions of ethical businesses will thus be freed from the tyranny of the few...

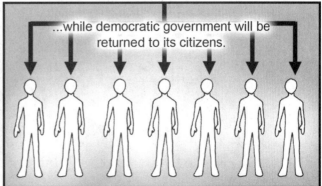

...while democratic government will be returned to its citizens.

 As Thomas Paine — another Pennsylvania resident — wrote on that 1776 December night and published two days before Christmas...

"Let it be told to the future world, that in the depth of winter, when nothing but hope and virtue could survive, that the city and the country, alarmed at one common danger, came forth to meet and repulse it."

FILLING THE TALK RADIO VACUUM

 There's a talk radio revolution going on, and it could give presidential adviser Karl Rove nightmares.

 It could mean the end of George W. Bush's seemingly unending ability to make biased assertions to the American people and not get called on them by the popular media.

A

B, C, D

Yes, mighty one...

A A

Liberal talk radio is blossoming. Air America Radio is well established throughout the country. Plus, my own syndicated program, which goes head-to-head in many markets with Rush Limbaugh, is growing by leaps and bounds. Even megacorp Clear Channel successfully carries my show on several of their stations.

 CLEARCHANNEL®

It's the nature of the marketplace to abhor a vacuum, and the hunger for liberal programming — as evidenced by its explosion across the Internet and its great success in the few markets where it can be found —

 — can be a very profitable vacuum to fill.

LEFT

POP!

At the same time, right-wing hosts are fading. For example, Bill O'Reilly's radio failures in Limbaugh-dominated markets, documented by Internet journalist Matt Drudge (creator of the Drudge Report), imply the obvious: right-wing talk radio has reached market saturation and is no longer a growth industry.

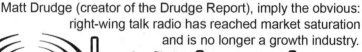

According to Geoff Metcalf on WorldNetDaily.com, the O'Reilly show is even paying stations — in one case over a quarter of a million dollars — to continue to carry the show.

PLEEEEEASE!

≈Sigh≈ I *guess* we'll carry you...

The demands of the huge unserved market of Democratic voters and progressives are real, and Internet empires are being built on them.

We want liberal radio!

Okay! Okay!

For example, www.radiopower.org recently announced that their progressive Internet talk radio network has surpassed the 1.5 million-user mark.

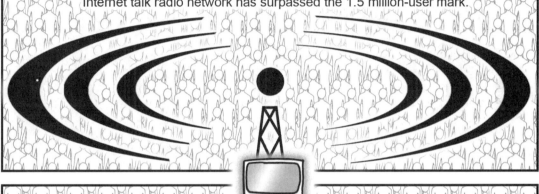

While still in its formative stages, Internet radio is fueling a new wave of effective, targeted communication, generating audience numbers that are attracting serious industry attention and creating programming that is increasingly being syndicated to terrestrial radio stations.

The strongly left-leaning *Democracy Now* radio show has exploded in listenership.

Although the right-wing talkers love to claim that they

simply balance National Public Radio

it's an argument that commercial programmers know is specious.

NPR never has and never will run hour after hour of a single commentator ranting about the wonders of one party and the horrors of another.

...and now for another solid hour of pure biased talk radio...

Centrist and left-wing talk radio is still an emerging product with a huge unserved market.

Is it safe to listen to the radio again?

And, with right-wing ideologues now in charge of our government, the time has never been better.

As Rush Limbaugh showed during the Clinton years (the peak of his success), "issues" talk thrives best in an underdog environment.

The bigger they are, the more targets they have!

It's in the American psyche to give a fair listen to people challenging the party in power.

Get ready for liberal/progressive talk radio, coming to a commercial station near you!*

THE SECOND AMERICAN REVOLUTION

Many Americans believe that the Draconian Patriot Act and the proposed "improvements" in Patriot II are totally new in the experience of America and may spell the end of both democracy and the Bill of Rights.

History and current events offer us both warnings and hope.

TYRANNY

Bill of Rights

1798   2004

Although you won't learn much about it from reading the histories of the Founders that are promoted in the corporate media these days, the most notorious stain on the presidency of John Adams began in 1798...

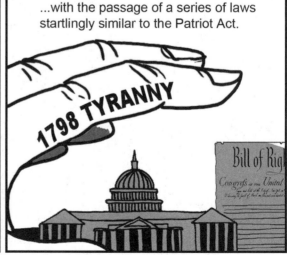

...with the passage of a series of laws startlingly similar to the Patriot Act.

1798 TYRANNY

Bill of Rig

It started when Benjamin Franklin Bache, grandson of Benjamin Franklin and editor of the Philadelphia newspaper, *Aurora*, began to speak out against the policies of then-President John Adams.

Bache supported Vice President* Thomas Jefferson's Democratic-Republican Party (today called the Democratic Party)...

1798

...at a time when John Adams led the conservative Federalists (who would be philosophically identical to today's GOP Republicans).

Bache attacked Adams in an editorial piece, calling the president...

"old, querulous, Bald, blind, crippled, Toothless Adams."

To be sure, Bache wasn't the only one attacking Adams in 1798. His *Aurora* was one of about 20 independent newspapers aligned with Jefferson's Democratic-Republicans, and many were openly questioning Adams' policies and ridiculing Adams' fondness for formality and grandeur.

On the Federalist side, conservative newspaper editors were equally outspoken.

Noah Webster wrote that Jefferson's Democratic-Republicans were...

"the refuse, the sweepings of the most depraved part of mankind from the most corrupt nations on earth."

Another Federalist characterized the Democratic-Republicans as...

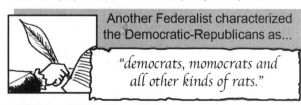

"democrats, momocrats and all other kinds of rats."

Meanwhile Federalist newspapers worked hard to turn the rumor of Jefferson's relationship with his deceased wife's half-sister, slave Sally Hemings, into a full-blown scandal.

* Before 1804 and the passage of the 12th Amendment, the vice-president was the runner-up in the presidential election and not necessarily from the same party.

University of Missouri-Rolla history professor Larry Gragg points out in an October 1998 article in *American History* magazine that, while Jefferson and his Demo-Republicans had learned to develop a thick skin, Bache's writings sent Adams and his wife into a self-righteous frenzy.

Adams' wife Abigail felt that Bache was expressing the "malice" of a man possessed by Satan. The Democratic-Republican editors were engaging, she said, in "abuse, deception, and falsehood," and Bache was a "lying wretch."

You can't talk like that about *me*!

She insisted that her husband and Congress must punish Bache for his "most insolent and abusive" words about her husband and his administration. His "wicked and base, violent and calumniating abuse" must be stopped.

Abigail Adams followed the logic employed by modern-day conservatives who call the administration "the government" and say that those opposed to an administration's policies are "unpatriotic."

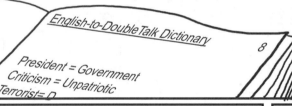

English-to-DoubleTalk Dictionary

President = Government
Criticism = Unpatriotic
Terrorist = D

8

She wrote that the "abuse" being "leveled against the Government" of the United States (her husband) could even plunge the nation into a "civil war."

Worked into a frenzy by Abigail Adams and Federalist newspapers of the day, Federalist senators and congressmen — who controlled both legislative houses along with the presidency — came to the defense of John Adams by passing a series of four laws that came to be known together as the Alien and Sedition Acts.

Alien and Sedition Acts

The vote on the acts was so close — 44 to 41 in the House of Representatives —

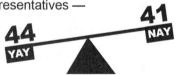

44 YAY

41 NAY

— that in order to ensure passage the lawmakers wrote a sunset (expiration) provision into its most odious parts. Those laws, unless renewed, would expire the last day of John Adams' first term of office, March 3, 1801.

Good Thru: 03/03/1801

Empowered with this early version of the Patriot Act, President John Adams ordered his "unpatriotic" opponents arrested...

...and specified that judges on the Supreme Court — all Federalists, thanks to stacking by Washington and Adams — would be both judges (supervising the trials) *and* jurors (deciding the outcomes).

Bache was the first to be hauled into jail (even before the laws became effective!), followed by *New York Time Piece* editor John Daly Burk, whose paper promptly went out of business. Bache died of yellow fever while awaiting trial. Burk accepted deportation to avoid imprisonment.

Others didn't avoid prison so easily. Editors of seventeen of the twenty or so Democratic-Republican-affiliated newspapers were arrested, and ten were convicted and imprisoned. Many of their newspapers went out of business.

Bache's successor, William Duane, continued the attacks on Adams. In the June 24, 1799, issue of the *Aurora* he published a private letter in which then-Vice President Adams admitted that there were still men influenced by Great Britain in the U.S. government.

The letter cast Adams in an embarrassing light, as it implied that Adams himself might still have British loyalties (something suspected by many, ever since his pre-revolutionary defense of British soldiers involved in the Boston Massacre).

Grrrrrr...

The quick-tempered Adams was furious.

Imprisoning his opponents in the press was only the beginning for Adams,

FREE SPEECH

Knowing Jefferson would mount a challenge to his presidency in 1800, he and the Federalists hatched a plot to pass secret legislation that would, in case of "emergency," allow the Supreme Court to overrule the Electoral College and decide disputed presidential elections "behind closed doors."

Duane got evidence of the plot and exposed it.

Aurora

EXTRA!! EXTRA!!
Adams' Conspiracy!

TYRANNY

POWER

It was altogether too much for the president, who didn't want to let go of his power...

Adams had Duane arrested and hauled before Congress on Sedition Act charges.

Duane would have stayed in jail had not Vice President Thomas Jefferson intervened, letting Duane leave to "consult his attorney."

Duane went into hiding until the end of the Adams presidency.

The Alien and Sedition Acts reflected the new attitude Adams and his wife had brought to Washington D.C. in 1796: a take-no-prisoners type of politics in which no opposition was tolerated.

Now Entering Washington D.C.

Opposition

America's second president succeeded in **creating an atmosphere of fear and division in the new republic, and it brought out the worst in his conservative supporters.**

Across the new nation, Federalist mobs and Federalist-controlled police and militia attacked Democratic-Republican newspapers and shouted down or threatened individuals who dared speak out in public against John Adams.

Even members of Congress were not legally immune from the long arm of Adams' Alien and Sedition Acts.

The Federalists already hated Vermont's Congressman Matthew Lyon for his opposition to the law.

He was even caned in Congress by irate Federalist Roger Griswold.

 Finally, Lyon wrote an article pointing out Adams'

"continual grasp for power"

and suggested that Adams had an

"unbounded thirst for ridiculous pomp, foolish adulation, and selfish avarice".

 Federalists convened a grand jury and indicted the congressman for bringing...

"the President and government of the United States into contempt."

Lyon, who had served in the Continental Army during the Revolutionary War, was led through the town of Vergennes, Vermont, in shackles.

He ran for re-election from his 12x16-foot Vergennes jail cell and handily won his seat.

Vermont loves you Matt!

Lyon wrote from jail to his constituents:

"It is quite a new kind of jargon to call a Representative of the People an Opposer of the Government because he does not, as a legislator, advocate and acquiesce in every proposition that comes from the Executive."

Which brings us to today.

The end of the story of Adams' attempts to thwart the Bill of Rights and turn the United States into a one-party state offers hope for those who oppose similar efforts of the George W. Bush or any other autocratic administration.

The furor over the Alien and Sedition Acts made the Democratic-Republican newspapers more popular than ever.

Get'm while they're hot!

In like fashion, progressive websites and talk shows are today proliferating across the Internet, and victims of illegal arrests at anti-Bush rallies are often featured on the Web and on radio programs like *Democracy Now*.

The day Adams signed the Acts, Thomas Jefferson left town in protest. Even though Jefferson was Vice President and could theoretically benefit from using the acts against his own political enemies, he and James Madison continued to protest and work against them.

Founding Fathers on Strike!

Founding Fathers on Str

Jefferson wrote the text for a non-binding resolution against the acts that was adopted by the Kentucky legislature...

...and James Madison wrote one for the Virginia legislature.

Today, in similar fashion, over 160 communities across America have adopted resolutions against Bush's Patriot Act...

PATRIOT ACT

...and, in the spirit of Matthew Lyon, Vermont Congressman Bernie Sanders has introduced legislation to repeal parts of the act.

Jefferson beat Adams in the election of 1800 as a wave of voter revulsion over Adams' phony and self-serving "patriotism" swept over the nation...

◆ 1800 ◆
"The Bloodless Revolution"

...along with concerns about Adams' belligerent war rhetoric against the French.

Federalists

These days, citizens of all political persuasions have become appalled by both...

...the invasion of Iraq...

...and the excesses of the Patriot Act.

There's a growing conviction that liberals/progressives can once again be victorious over conservatives.

When Jefferson exposed Adams as a poseur and tool of the powerful elite, the rot within Adams' Federalist Party was exposed along with it.

The Federalists lost their hold on Congress in the election of 1800 and began a 30-year slide into total disintegration...

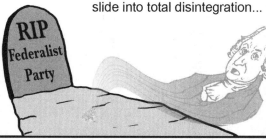

RIP Federalist Party

...later to be reincarnated...

I'm a Fed...

...er...

...as Whigs...

I'm a Whi...

...and then...

...er...

...as Republicans.

I'm a Republican!

Today, the rot in the Republican Party is more and more obvious.

Is there something on my back?

Elitist... Kick me!

As bribery scandals proliferate...

...tax cuts for the rich are understood for what they are...

...and average citizens become more and more alarmed at the corporate takeover of America.

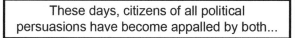

145

Americans are demanding the kind of representation for We the People that non-DLC Democrats, Greens, and other progressives can offer.

In what came to be known as "The Revolution of 1800" or "The Second American Revolution," Thomas Jefferson freed all the men imprisoned by Adams as one of his first acts of office.

Jefferson even gave back the fines they'd paid — with interest — and granted them formal pardons and apologies.

...and here's a little extra for your troubles...

Thanks TJ!

Today, undoing the Patriot Act and kicking corporate money out of Washington D.C. have become popular progressive and Democratic campaign themes.

The history of John Adams' failed presidency gives encouragement and hope to those committed to real democracy and genuine freedom.

Constitution

Bill of Rights
Congress of the United States.

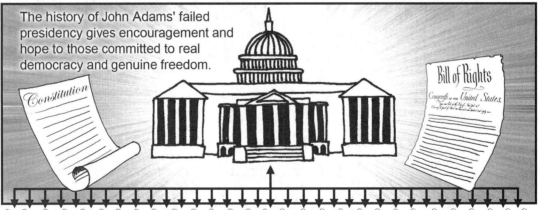

History shows *that when enough people become politically active, they can rescue the soul of America* from sliding into a corrupt, abusive police state.

The future of our nation is now at risk just as much as it was in 1800.

It's time to wake up and work to elect and empower politicians who will support real democracy.

If we're successful, America may experience a revival every bit as extraordinary as that brought about by Jefferson's Second American Revolution.

Can we do it in time?!

Yes, by becoming truly politically active and by letting those who're sitting on the fence know that — this time — it really matters. This is not just a single, out-of-control administration that has to be purged.

It's a historical call to Americans to live up to the promise of our visionary Founders...

...and, perhaps for the first time, establish a government of, by and for We the People.

Most importantly, we can't just vent our frustrations. We have to act now with wisdom and focus, to dismantle the new corporatocracy and restore a constitutionally-limited democratic republic to America.

TAKING BACK AMERICA

In his memoirs, Barry Goldwater said...

"We have arrived at our present position of peril in the world and at home because our leaders have refused to tell us the truth. ... **If the Republic is to survive, we must find and follow new leaders.**"

Another traditional conservative Arizona Senator, John McCain, echoed those sentiments in a July 11, 2002 speech on corporate leadership. He told the National Press Club...

"Threats to our greatness come not just from foreign enemies and alien ideologies that hold our ideals in contempt. ... They also come from those few among us who perceive their self-interest as separate from the interests of our society, who in their selfish pursuits abjure the values of honesty, fairness and patriotism, and threaten to damage the very trust that makes freedom work."

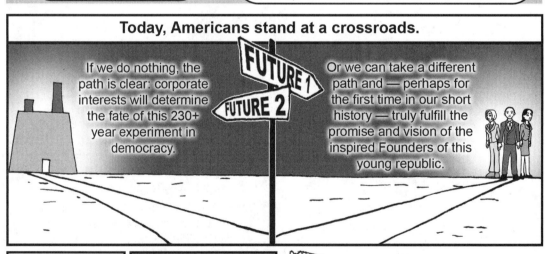

Today, Americans stand at a crossroads.

If we do nothing, the path is clear: corporate interests will determine the fate of this 230+ year experiment in democracy.

FUTURE 1

FUTURE 2

Or we can take a different path and — perhaps for the first time in our short history — truly fulfill the promise and vision of the inspired Founders of this young republic.

Do we acquiesce?...

What's the use?

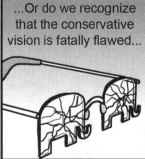

...Or do we recognize that the conservative vision is fatally flawed...

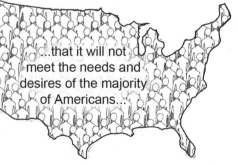

...that it will not meet the needs and desires of the majority of Americans...

...and will lead to aristocracy and feudalism...

...instead of democracy?

Do we continue to allow our rights to be trampled and our choices usurped by transnational corporations...

...with their awesome financial power...

...and their political servants?

Or do we take back the country that belongs to all of us?

Do we have the courage to commit to the revolutionary rebirthing of America based on solid principles like liberty, justice, compassion, fairness, honesty, authenticity...

Bill of Rights
Congress of the United States.

...cooperation, mutual empowerment, whole-system thinking, ecological and economic sustainability, meaningful education and work, personal and global health and vitality...

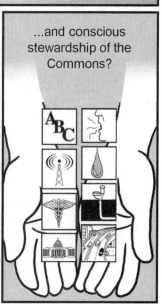

...and conscious stewardship of the Commons?

I hope and pray so.

If we choose to do so, how do we replace the vision that is presently driving the government and the nation?

What are the feasible strategies?

How do we remove a government of blatant "neo-cons"...

...and not settle for one with a less harsh exterior but a similar core agenda — what could be called "neo-con lite"?

Gimme a hug!

The Democratic Leadership Council is financed by many of the same backers as the Bush administration.

Do the corporate interest boogie!

May I lead?

They dance to many of the same tunes.

DLC members following the agendas of their funders still cost Americans decent-wage jobs and entrepreneurial opportunities...

I support *Click* this issue!

...and their support for corporate-driven globalization and overseas military adventures create the same tragic human consequences around the planet.

What effective actions can we take?

For one thing, we can follow the lead of a number of municipalities across the country and begin limiting corporate powers and rescinding corporate personhood.

In urging our local representatives to take action...

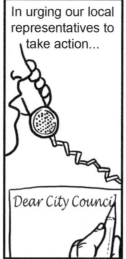

Dear City Council

...we can also present them with sample non-binding resolutions that are much easier to pass.

These critical strategies are outlined in Appendix B. Please read that section if you feel the impulse to "answer the call" put forth here.

Honest, successful change movements always work from the bottom up, not the top down.

As Margaret Mead put it:

"Never doubt that a small group of thoughtful, committed citizens can change the world; Indeed, it's the only thing that ever has."

Leaders and elected officials usually don't just wake up one day and change.

Eureka!

Change your policy!

Support your people! Change Now!

Support your people

Citizens push them to do so.

This is how it worked with the abolition and suffrage movements of a century ago...

VOTES FOR WOMEN

...and with late 20th century movements like those for:

civil rights

women's rights

and the 1990s Americans with Disabilities Act

...among others.

Activists wrote...

books, articles, and editorials.

They formed citizens' groups...

...and challenged laws.

Often they were harassed and sometimes arrested.

Political parties eventually staked out positions.

Communities passed resolutions and laws.

Resolution

Advocacy groups worked for constitutional amendments...

Amendment to the Constitution

...or helped bring supportive legal cases to the Supreme Court.

Whichever way the process of returning corporations to their former status ultimately happens...

RIGHTS

PRIVILEGES

...it'll only come about when a critical mass of the electorate realizes it's an issue.

That sounds great, but we can't really wait for that to unfold, can we?

No, we don't have the time. So, let's look at other pieces of the puzzle we could put into place sooner.

How are those of us who believe in this new vision —

— most standing on the outside of government, looking in — to deal with...

...oil wars...

...endemic corporate cronyism...

...slashed environmental regulations...

...corporate-controlled voting machines...

...the devastation of America's natural areas...

...the fouling of our air and waters...

...and an administration that daily gives the pharmaceutical, HMO, banking, and insurance industries whatever they want regardless of how many people are harmed?

This lack of political power is a crisis that others have faced before. We could learn from their experience.

After Barry Goldwater's crushing defeat in the 1964 presidential election, a similar crisis faced a loose coalition of..

| gun lovers | abortion foes | southern segregationists | Ayn Rand libertarians | "Moonies" |

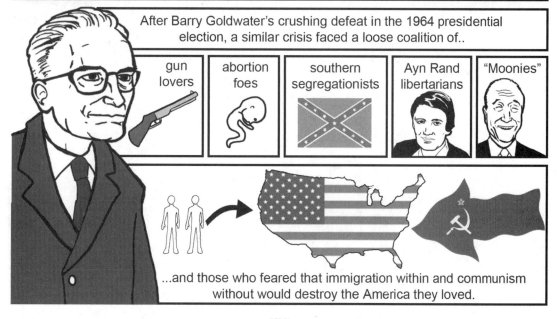

...and those who feared that immigration within and communism without would destroy the America they loved.

Each of these various groups had tried their own "direct action" tactics: from demonstrations, to pamphleteering, to organizing, to fielding candidates.

None had succeeded in gaining mainstream recognition or affecting American political processes.

If anything, their efforts had instead led to their being branded as special interest or fringe groups, which further diminished their political power.

So the conservatives decided not to get angry, but to get power.

Led by Joseph Coors and a handful of other ultra-rich funders, they decided the only way to seize control of the American political agenda was to infiltrate and take over one of the two national political parties...

...using their own think tanks like the Coors-funded Heritage Foundation to mold public opinion along the way.

Now they regularly get their spokespeople on radio and television talk shows and newscasts — even NPR — and write a steady stream of daily op-ed pieces for national newspapers.

They launched an aggressive takeover of Dwight Eisenhower's still mostly "moderate" Republican Party...

...opening up the "big tent" to invite in groups that had previously been considered on the fringe.

Archconservative neo-Christians who argue the Bible should replace the Constitution even funded the startup of a corporation to manufacture computer-controlled voting machines, which are now installed across the nation.

And leader of the Unification Church and self-proclaimed messiah Reverend Moon took over *The Washington Times* newspaper and the national news service, United Press International (UPI).

THE WASHINGTON TIMES

Their efforts have borne fruit, as Kevin Phillips predicted they would in his prescient 1969 book...

The Emerging Republican Majority

...and as David Brock so well documents in his book...

Blinded by the Right

But the sweet victory of the conservatives in capturing control of the Republican Party — and thus of American politics — has turned bitter in the mouths of the average American and others around the world.

Ewww...

America now faces:

staggering deficits

an eviscerated Social Security system

"voluntary" pollution controls

war for oil

federal benches stacked with right-wing ideologues

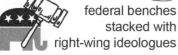

bellicose nationalist foreign policies

and the handing over of much of the infrastructure of governance to multinational corporate campaign donors.

The conservative vision has brought a vast devastation to the nation, nearly destroyed the entrepreneurial American dream...

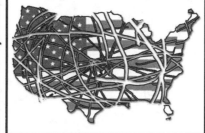

...and caused the rest of the world to view us with shock and horror.

What the heck is going on over there?!

Thus, many progressives are suggesting that it's time for concerned Americans to reclaim Thomas Jefferson's Democratic Party.

It may, in fact, be our only short-term hope to avoid a final total fascistic takeover of America...

...and a third world war.

But wait!

say the Greens and Progressives, some Democrats, and left-leaning Reform Party members.

The mainstream Democrats are just weaker versions of the Republicans!

True enough, in many cases.

And it hasn't been working for them, because, as Democrat Harry Truman said...

"When voters are given a choice between voting for a Republican or a Democrat who acts like a Republican, they'll vote for the Republican every time."

(And, history shows, voters are equally uninterested in Republicans who act like Democrats.)

Alternative parties have an important place in American politics, and those in them should continue to work for their strength and vitality.

Green Party

Libertarian Party

Reform Party

They're essential as incubators of ideas and nexus points for activism.

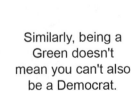

Those on the right learned this lesson well: many groups that in the past fielded their own candidates (such as Pat Robertson) are now still intact but have also become powerful influencers of the Republican Party.

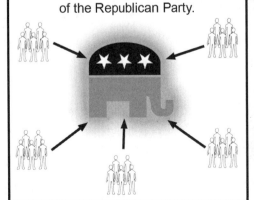

Similarly, being a Green doesn't mean you can't also be a Democrat.

This is not a popular truth.

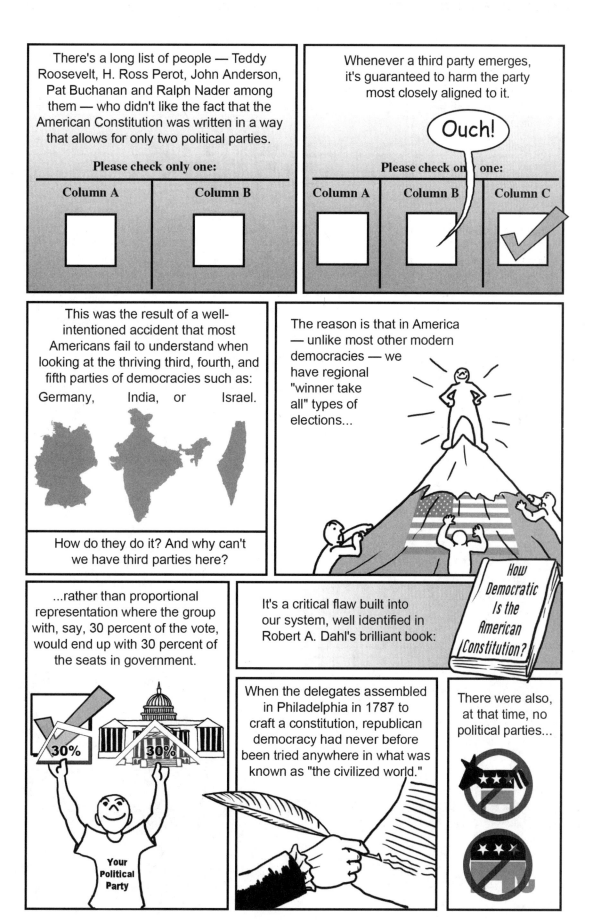

There's a long list of people — Teddy Roosevelt, H. Ross Perot, John Anderson, Pat Buchanan and Ralph Nader among them — who didn't like the fact that the American Constitution was written in a way that allows for only two political parties.

Please check only one:

Column A	Column B

Whenever a third party emerges, it's guaranteed to harm the party most closely aligned to it.

Ouch!

Please check only one:

Column A	Column B	Column C
		✓

This was the result of a well-intentioned accident that most Americans fail to understand when looking at the thriving third, fourth, and fifth parties of democracies such as:

Germany, India, or Israel.

How do they do it? And why can't we have third parties here?

The reason is that in America — unlike most other modern democracies — we have regional "winner take all" types of elections...

...rather than proportional representation where the group with, say, 30 percent of the vote, would end up with 30 percent of the seats in government.

30%   30%

Your Political Party

It's a critical flaw built into our system, well identified in Robert A. Dahl's brilliant book:

How Democratic Is the American Constitution?

When the delegates assembled in Philadelphia in 1787 to craft a constitution, republican democracy had never before been tried anywhere in what was known as "the civilized world."

There were also, at that time, no political parties...

...and "father of the Constitution" James Madison warned loudly in *Federalist* #10 against the emergence of parties.

In part, Madison issued his warning because he knew that the system they were creating would, in the presence of political parties, rapidly become far less democratic.

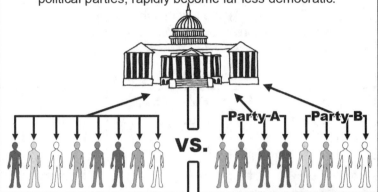

Party-A   Party-B

VS.

In the regional winner-take-all type of elections the Framers wrote into the Constitution, the loser in a two-party race — even if s/he had fully 49.9 percent of the vote — would end up with no voice whatsoever.

49.9%

And, ironically, the combined losers in a 3-way or 4-way race could even be the candidates or parties whose overall positions were most closely embraced by the majority of the people.

WINNER
40%

30%   30%

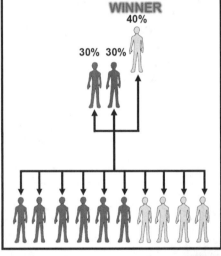

But what to do?

In 1787 the best solution to this unfairness was to speak out against the formation of political parties or

"factions"

...as Madison did at length and in several venues.

This idea didn't last long, however.

Within a decade of the Constitution's ratification, Jefferson's split with Adams had led to the emergence of two strong political parties...

...and the problems Madison foresaw began and are with us to this day.

This is particularly problematic in presidential elections.

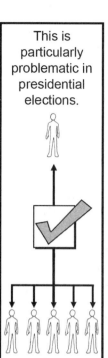

Some suggest that H. Ross Perot's participation in the 1992 election drew enough votes away from the elder George Bush that Bill Clinton won without a true majority.

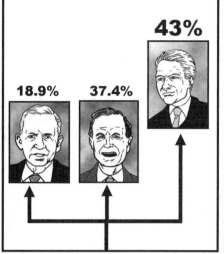

18.9% 37.4% **43%**

Similarly, Ralph Nader's participation in the 2000 election drew enough votes away from Al Gore that it was easy for the controversial handling of Florida votes to tip the electoral scales in favor of his brother, George.

2.7% **48.4%** **47.9%**

Conservative activists recognized this inherent flaw in the electoral system of the United States and decided to capitalize on it.

If you press right here...

Avoiding the third party pitfall, they took over the Republican Party...

...and then successfully seized control of the government of the United States of America with Ronald Reagan and his infamous "kitchen cabinet."

As we can see by comparing the vision of the 1990s Project for a New American Century with the invasion and occupation of Iraq, these once-marginalized conservative ideologues are the real power behind Bush's foreign policy.

Liberals weren't so practically minded. Instead of:

LIBERAL

funding think tanks to influence public opinion

subsidizing radio and TV talk show hosts nationwide

and working to take over the Democratic Party...

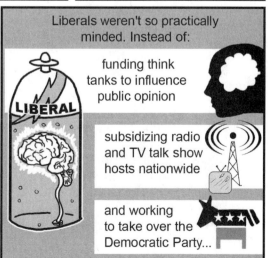

159

...many left to create their own parties.

Let's make a **new** party for people as idealistic as us!

Others gave up on mainstream politics altogether.

The remaining Democrats were caught in the awkward position of having to try to embrace the same corporate donors as the Republicans, although they weren't anywhere near as successful as Republicans because they hadn't (and haven't) so fully sold out to corporate and wealthy interests.

Now what am I supposed to do?

Come here a sec...

We see the result in races across the nation, such as my state of Vermont.

In the 2002 election for governor and lieutenant governor, the people who voted for the Democratic and Progressive candidates constituted a clear majority.

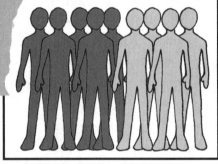

Nonetheless, the Republican candidates became Governor and Lieutenant Governor with 45 percent and 41 percent of the vote respectively because each had more votes than his Democratic or Progressive opponents alone.

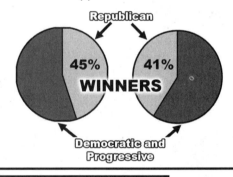

Republican

45%   41%

WINNERS

Democratic and Progressive

Similarly, Republicans have used liberal and progressive third-party participation to their advantage. In a July 12, 2002, story in the *Washington Post* ("GOP Figure Behind Greens Offer, N.M. Official Says"), Thomas B. Edsall wrote:

"The chairman of the Republican Party of New Mexico said yesterday he was approached by a GOP figure who asked him to offer the state Green Party at least $100,000 to run candidates in two contested congressional districts in an effort to divide the Democratic vote."

The Republicans well understand — and carefully use — the fact that in the American electoral system a third-party candidate will always harm the major-party candidate with whom s/he is most closely aligned.

Quit messing up my game!

But I'm proving a point!

So, are there options?

160

The Australians solved this problem in the last decade by instituting a nationwide system of modified **instant run-off voting (IRV)**, a system that is beginning to find favor in communities across the United States.

IRV enables voters to rank the candidates 1, 2, 3, etc., which results in more positive campaigns...

...and more fair, balanced and accurate representation of the political spectrum.

http://www.fairvote.org/irv/

There are also efforts to reform our electoral system along the lines of other democratic nations by instituting **proportional representation** systems such as that first proposed by John Stuart Mill in 1861...

...and now adopted by virtually every democracy in the world except the U.S., Australia, Greece, the United Kingdom, and Canada.

This process produces more choices and more competition among ideas and issues...

...and increases voter turnout.

Most importantly, it more fully represents America's increasingly diverse population in the halls of government because it's based on a fair-share model rather than winner take all.

http://www.fairvote.org/pr/

Another initiative that's gaining steam in cities and states across America is the move toward public financing of elections.

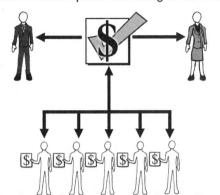

Because it's fueled by grassroots vigor, it has high chances of success down the road.

On its website, Common Cause outlines the tremendous potential of public financing:

It reduces the corrupting influence of special interest contributions on our political process.

It provides those without access to great wealth the opportunity to run for public office — one of the highest callings in our democracy.

RICH   **POOR**

It reduces the overwhelming fundraising advantage incumbents enjoy over challengers.

INCUMBENT   **CHALLENGER**

It helps restore faith in democracy and our public institutions.

"Honest Politician" is no longer an oxymoron!

www.commoncause.org/fairelectionsSF/why.html

We already have a public financing mechanism for presidential elections (the check-off box on federal tax returns)...

Cough! Cough!

...but that seems doomed to failure, thanks to George W. Bush's incredible "money machine," that enabled him to opt out of voluntary public financing during the 2000 primaries.

Up to that point, all presidential candidates had played by the rules since 1976.

Bush's unprecedented move was strategically sound: while Al Gore was limited to around $45 million in public funding, Bush's cash cow pumped out $101 million —

$45 Million

$101 Million

— more than all the private money raised by Republican presidential nominees since Watergate, after adjusting for inflation.

$$$$

With a goal of raising at least $170 million before the GOP national convention in 2004, Bush has once more shunned public funds...

MORE!

...and has forced some leading Democratic candidates to opt out as well.

That's just gross.

So, where's the hope?

Though this particular reform will not produce results overnight, the initial indications are heartening.

Already, Maine, Arizona, Massachusetts, Vermont, North Carolina, New Mexico, New York City, Los Angeles and San Francisco have passed some form of public financing scheme.

(Go to Appendix C for more details on this.)

As citizens, many of us need to get over our aversion to giving "taxpayers money" to politicians.

I dunno...

If we appreciate that this only would be a tiny percentage of the tens of billions that corporate-influenced politicians waste each year in the current system — and could insure clean elections — the choice becomes clear.

Please! Take it!

Do we maintain our dysfunctional system that produces mediocre or destructive results...

...or do we replace it with one more likely to elect the best person for the job...

...the person who's only political loyalty and responsibility is to We the People?

This is exciting, but will any of these reforms really help?

Yes, these are good and important efforts for the long-term future of American democracy.

2004

But they won't happen in time to influence the 2004 elections, and we're facing a crisis right now.

There are a few Democratic stalwarts who oppose the Bush administration on the national stage...

...but while the rest of us remain fixated on the nightly news, conservatives have crept into the very heart of Jefferson's Party.

I'm a rare breed of donkey...

You don't look familiar.

Thus, the best immediate solution to advance the progressive agenda is for progressives to join and take back the Democratic Party in the same way conservatives seized control of the Republican Party, starting in 1964.

As the first attack of Baghdad began in March, 2003, I thought about how the Democratic Party might change if most of the protesters in the streets were to join the Democratic Party and run for leadership positions in their local town or county.

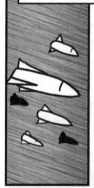

NO BLOOD FOR OIL!

NO WAR

In short order, a reborn Democratic Party could become a powerful force for progressive principles and democracy in America and the world, maybe even in time to influence the 2004 election.

But don't misunderstand.

While the Democratic Party strategy offers us the greatest and quickest payoff, I would hope that our brothers and sisters in the GOP — many of whom are concerned and even alarmed about the direction this country is headed in — would also work to reform and help steer the Republican Party back from their anti-democratic tendencies.

There's actually far more that unites us Democrats, dissatisfied Republicans, Independents and Greens than divides us.

We need to find a common cause and break the nasty cycle of polarization.

As the invasion of Iraq got underway, I began receiving a string of e-mails expressing despair, fear, or panic.

I began answering them by saying...

From: "Thom Hartmann" <www.thomhartmann.com>
Subject: The Real American War Against Oppression

"The nation I love is confronting a crisis no smaller than those faced by Roosevelt, Lincoln, and Washington...

...a crisis that will determine if American democracy survives to the next generation.

We may not be able to instantly arrest the slide of our democracy into a new kind of feudalism, but we can begin by exercising our political rights and replacing the corporate cheerleaders, the politicians for hire and other elected officials unresponsive to We the People."

But what about the corporate-controlled media?

That was the same problem faced by the Christian Right 25 years ago, when all the coverage they could get was of Tammy Faye Bakker scandals.

But once they'd taken over the Republican Party, the press could no longer ignore them, and Pat Robertson and Jerry Falwell are now regulars on network TV.

Another person answered my now-form e-mail by saying:

"I want to participate in producing a detailed plan for the future of America, rather than just joining a corrupt and tired-out political party."

My response was that if there were enough of us in the Democratic Party, it could become a cleaned-up and powerful activist force. It's possible: just look at how the anti-abortion and gun-lovin' folks took over the once-moribund Republican Party.

Another said:

"But what about their rigged computer-controlled voting machines?"

My answer is that only a political party as large and resourceful as the Democrats could have the power to re-institute exit polling...

...ensure that auditable paper trails are left by computer voting machines...

...and catch scams like...

...the voter-list purges Jeb Bush used to steal the 2000 and 2002 elections for himself and his brother...

...and that apparently stole the Georgia election from Sen. Max Cleland.

But the Democratic Party can do it only if we, in massive numbers, join it, embrace it, and ultimately gain a powerful and decisive voice in its policy-making and selection of candidates.

167

It's time to wake up and work to elect and empower politicians interested in true democracy.

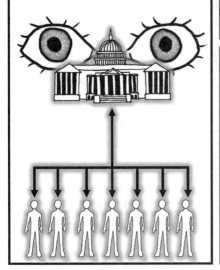

To make a success of this New American Revolution it's going to require all of us pitching in.

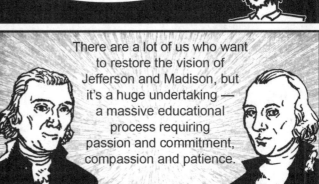

There are a lot of us who want to restore the vision of Jefferson and Madison, but it's a huge undertaking — a massive educational process requiring passion and commitment, compassion and patience.

When we publicly re-examine specific threads of the social fabric, it helps our society at large to reframe its perceptions...

...and begin seeing certain existing patterns as being at odds with our core values.

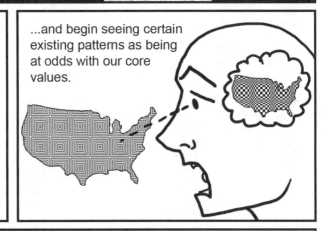

Each of us who really cares about the future of our country needs to step up and become a grassroots activist for democracy.

APATHY

ACTIVISM

The actions proposed in this book transcend narrow political and social causes. Each of us can reach out to established organizations or find other ways to link with those who want change.

Enter Trail Here

POLITICAL LANDSCAPE

Each of us can collect signatures supporting a local resolution.

Each of us can meet with individual city council members or county commissioners, with state representatives and senators.

This is what paid lobbyists do all the time and, like them, we can offer specific legislative language to our representatives.

We can work together to make both the public and public officials aware of the theft of democracy that has been going on since 1886 and has been accelerating in recent years.

Each of us can contact the local branch of the Democratic Party...

Go Donkeys!

...and become an active participant, connecting with like-minded folks and articulating a new vision for a party that has lost its way.

Remember! We are not alone. There is a huge demographic of people who care deeply about much in their lives...

YOU

...but who feel alienated from the political circus and don't bother to vote.

Sigh

(For example, see the work of Paul H. Ray and Sherry Ruth Anderson on their website, www.culturalcreatives.org)

In fact, about half of all eligible voters do not vote in presidential elections, partly because they feel it's a futile exercise.

What's the use?

The contentious 2000 election and the Bush administration's subsequent performance have acutely demonstrated the consequences of our choices.

The Bush administration's gift is to help awaken the apolitical, the cynical and the disillusioned.

Zzz

I can make a difference!

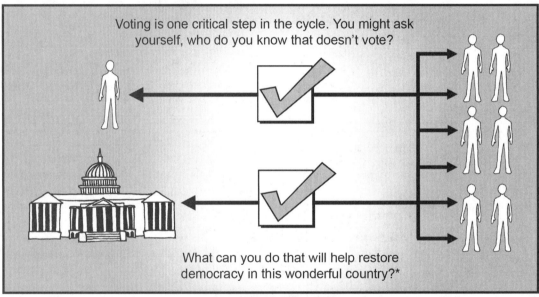

Voting is one critical step in the cycle. You might ask yourself, who do you know that doesn't vote?

What can you do that will help restore democracy in this wonderful country?*

As we put our hands and hearts into this New American Revolution, perhaps we should, as Jefferson, Madison and others did over 200 years ago, spell out our rights again as American citizens —

— this time in a

21st Century

context.

Here are my ideas for a new declaration that, if embraced by enough of us, could restore the democracy that this nation's Founders intended:

Bill of Rights

Congress of the United States

* For current information on political action opportunities, visit www.we-the-people-book.com.

170

RESTORING DEMOCRACY
A Declaration of Rights for the 21st Century

I. Human Rights Are for Humans

Corporations are not persons.

We must update the 14th Amendment to insert "natural" before the word "persons"...

Amendment to the Constitution

...so corporations can no longer claim the "right to lie"...

...the "right to hide their crimes"...

...the "right to buy politicians and influence elections"...

....and "the right to force themselves on communities that don't want them."

Corporate charter laws should be amended on a state-by-state basis to reinstate the spirit of the Sherman Anti-Trust Act by again outlawing the ownership of one corporation by another...

...to limit the term of a corporation...

R.I.P.
Bob Corp
1913-2006

...to insert language requiring a corporation to place the needs of its community above its desire for profits, and, as Teddy Roosevelt so strongly urged us, to ban corporations from political activity of any sort.

Similarly, corporations are not nations and shouldn't stand on an equal footing with nations.

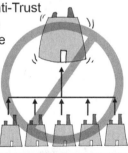

1

2

The United States should withdraw from support of treaties and agreements such as NAFTA, GATT, WTO, and its support of The World Bank.

II. We Own Our Government and Our Commons

"Drowning government in a bathtub" as the conservatives recommend may have been a good idea in the Soviet Union...

...but the United States is a constitutional representative democratic republic where our government is literally *us*.

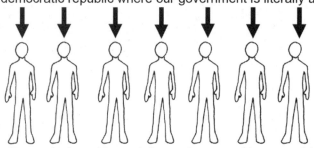

It was designed to work for us, be owned by us, exist solely by virtue of our ongoing approval, and answer to us.

Government functions must be transparent, and that transparency must also apply to corporations hired by government, particularly any who handle our votes.

The shared Commons of our nation — including our air, water, transportation routes, airwaves and cable networks, communication systems, military, police, prisons, fire services, health care, schools, infrastructure, and courts — must be held either by locally-controlled non-profit corporations or by government responsive to its citizens.

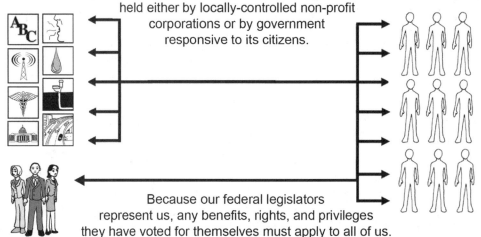

Because our federal legislators represent us, any benefits, rights, and privileges they have voted for themselves must apply to all of us.

Similarly, just as we must balance our budgets every year except when in a crisis, so must our governments.

Finally, government must not be a stepping-stone to private profiteering. We must re-institute laws against "revolving doors," particularly with regulatory agencies and the military and those they regulate or who provide military supplies.

III. In a Democratic Republic, Government Must Represent the Will of the Majority of the Citizens While Protecting the Rights of the Minorities

To make American government more democratic, we must join the rest of the world's modern democracies and institute either proportional representation or Instant Runoff Voting systems at local, state, and federal levels.

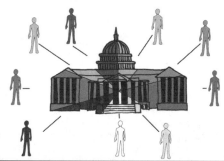

Similarly, human rights movements defending minorities and women against exploitation by corporate power structures or harm from paranoids, homophobes, and racists must be recognized, and the Equal Rights Amendment passed.

IV. A Strong Middle Class Is Vital to Democracy

In 1792, James Madison defined government's role in promoting an American middle class...

"by the silent operation of the laws, which, without violating the rights of property, reduce extreme wealth towards a state of mediocrity, and raise extreme indigence toward a state of comfort."

To say that somebody who earns millions a year by arbitrage works that much harder than a middle-class wage earner is simple nonsense.

We recommend restoring inflation-indexed income tax and inheritance tax rates to those that were extant from the 1930s to the 1960s — during the golden era of the American middle class.

We also recommend that government become the employer of last resort by taking on public works projects and supporting the arts, as it did during that era...

...and establishing a truly livable minimum wage.

V. Building a Civilization on Liquefied Fossils and Then Thinking It Will Last Forever Makes No Sense

According to British Petroleum, world oil reserves are enough to sustain us only into our children's lifetimes, and then will run out.

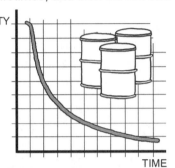

We must institute a Manhattan Project type of effort to create viable energy sources that are not dependent on fossil fuels, and, in the meantime, take immediate steps to reduce the use of and preserve our precious energy supplies before they're exhausted.

VI. We Are Part of Nature

The natural world — including the land, water, air and all living things — is our most vital and essential Commons...

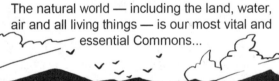

...and therefore must be protected from those who would despoil it for short-term profit.

As we poison the world, we cause human cancer epidemics and degrade our own quality of life.

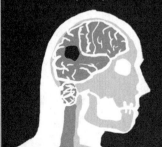

We — through our representative government — must take immediate steps to protect the Commons we share with all other life on planet Earth.

VII. Education is a Human Right, Regardless of Station of Birth

When Thomas Jefferson founded the University of Virginia, his vision was to provide a free education to every person interested in and capable of participating.

The Founders knew that classroom education is a right — and not a requirement — for life in a democracy.

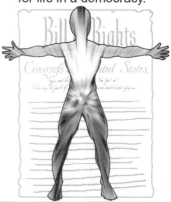

Therefore, university education should be free to all who academically qualify...

...and primary school education should neither be compulsory...

...nor should it be provided by for-profit corporations.

VIII. Health Care is a Human Right and Necessary to Sustain Freedom in a Democracy

America should join every other industrialized democracy in the world by instituting a single-payer health care system.

IX. America is not a Kingdom, and We Don't Elect Kings

To turn back from the "imperial presidency" and return the executive branch to its position co-equal with the other two branches of government...

...we recommend disbanding the primary instrument of presidential power, the Office Of Homeland Security —

— and requiring the President to meet weekly in open and public discussion with all members of Congress, as is done in the United Kingdom (i.e., "Prime Minister's Questions") and most other modern democracies.

X. The U.S. Government is an Instrument of Secular Democracy, not a Religious Theocracy, and Has No Right in Our Churches, Homes, or Bedrooms

What we do in private, among consenting adults, is our business and our business only.

Prostitution, drug abuse, alcoholism, and gambling addiction are medical and psychological problems, and thus should be handled by medical authorities.

All attempts to place these in the realm of the criminal justice system should be rescinded.

Similarly, the government has no right or business using the language or beliefs of any one of our many religions...

...or telling any of our religions what or how they should behave or believe.

THE CRITICAL AND DECISIVE HOUR

If we are to hold a vision of America that...

...doesn't depend on foreign sources of oil ...

...and doesn't require enormous expenditures of money and blood to project and protect empire...

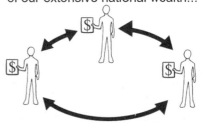

...if we are to preserve our planet for the Seventh Generation* and if we want a fair and equitable distribution of our extensive national wealth...

...simply protesting unnecessary wars...

NO BLOOD FOR OIL!

NO WAR

...the logging of old-growth forests...

SAVE OUR PLANET!

STOP TERRORISM AGAINST NATURE

...or tax cuts for the wealthy isn't enough.

NO BREAKS FOR THE RICH!

This means that ordinary citizens — even those who have never been involved before —

— must become political activists and spokespersons.

This means you **and** me!

*Some early Americans (the Six Nations Iroquois Confederacy) made decisions in light of the projected impacts on their descendants seven generations in the future.

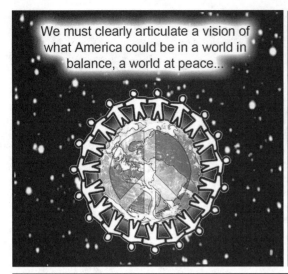
We must clearly articulate a vision of what America could be in a world in balance, a world at peace...

...and a world where the planet's vital natural resources are protected and renewed.

This is the ultimate family value, the highest patriotism, and the most desperately needed story to guide the next generation of Americans.

There is no quick fix.

If we're in this thing, we must be committed for the long term.

President John F. Kennedy said in his 1961 inaugural address...

"All this will not be finished in the first 100 days. Nor will it be finished in the first 1,000 days, nor in the life of this Administration, nor even perhaps in our lifetime on this planet. But let us begin."

Poet Ralph Waldo Emerson's words seem profoundly relevant at this time in America's history:

"One of the illusions [of life] is that the present hour is *not* the critical, decisive hour."

EPILOGUE:
BRINGING IT BACK HOME

Hey, Thom, you back from all your rabble rousing?

Yeah, Dave.

And, it's good to be home.

What've you got there?

Oh, it's the last part of the new book, Lin.

You two want to tell me what you think?

Sure!

THE RADICAL MIDDLE

Most Americans consider themselves neither right nor left, but independent and centrist.

LEFT   **RIGHT**

This is not a negative position, but is an emphatic statement that they don't buy into the extremist visions of either right or left.

Yet they know what they want, and have fought and died in wars from 1776 to the 20th century to preserve it.

They are the

LEFT   **RADICAL MIDDLE**   **RIGHT**

The founders of America explicitly defined the Radical Middle when they wrote in the Declaration of Independence:

*"We hold these truths to be self-evident, that all men are created equal, that they are endowed by their Creator with certain unalienable Rights, that among these are Life, Liberty and the pursuit of Happiness. That to secure these rights, Governments are instituted among Men, **deriving their just powers from the consent of the governed."***

This is the position of the Radical Middle:

That We the People, don't want governments or corporations running our lives.

We don't want a corporate state...

...*or* a police state.

We want back our democratic institutions...

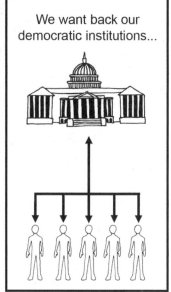

...a government again responsive to We the People...

...instead of today's government that has become captive to corporate special interests.

We want to live our lives in peace and security...

...but are neither willing to tolerate tyranny ...

...nor subject ourselves to a police state.

We want job security and safety in our old age...

...and have clearly seen that transnational corporations don't give a hoot about either.

We want a clean environment...

...and schools that inspire and fill our children with a thirst for knowledge.

And, we realize that the modern corporate-controlled state has let profit be more important than clean air or water...

...and that taking the cheap way out and just throwing more tests at our children kills rather than kindles their enthusiasm for learning.

High Score
High Score
High Score
High Score
High Score
High Score
High Score

We don't want a government bureaucracy or a corporate bureaucracy telling us what doctors we can see, but we do believe that a single-payer system funded by our taxes and administered by our government can work for all Americans.

We don't want to pay excessive taxes but we are also fully willing to pay our share for the upkeep of the nation, for safe streets and communities, and for our nation's defense.

We also, however, think that somebody who spends half their income on food and shelter shouldn't pay as much in taxes as somebody who has such a high income that food and shelter only represent a tiny fraction of their income.

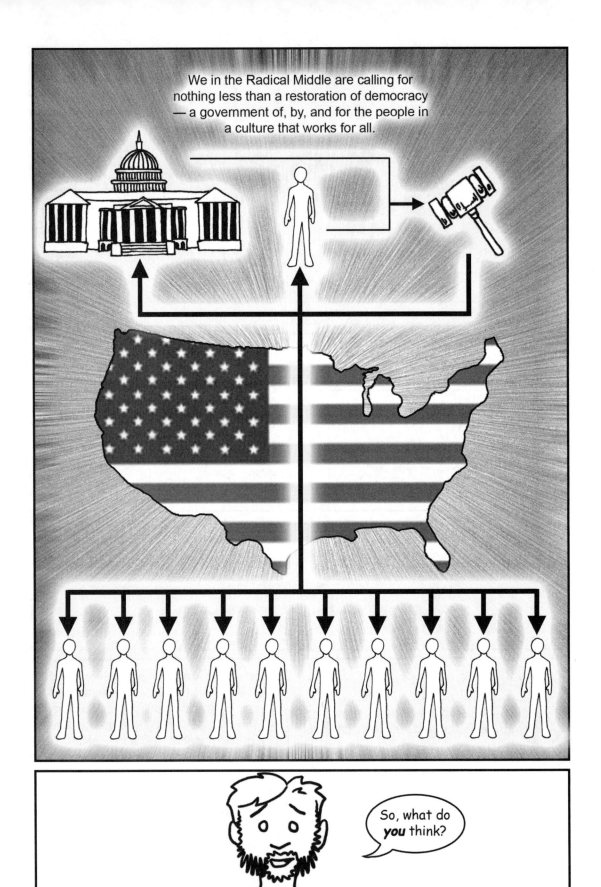

Wow! Never thought of myself as a radical, but you sure got me pegged!

Thom, that's really inspiring! And you know, I'd be more skeptical of our chances of success...

...if I didn't already know that only a third of the colonists supported the American Revolution...

Right. The critical population mass needed to make this political and cultural shift is not as large as one might think.

Here's what I've been finding in my travels:

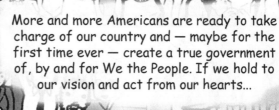

More and more Americans are ready to take charge of our country and — maybe for the first time ever — create a true government of, by and for We the People. If we hold to our vision and act from our hearts...

This *is* the critical, decisive hour.

★ ★ ★ ★ APPENDIX A: ★ ★ ★ ★
REFERENCES AND RESOURCES

The information in this appendix includes works cited, reference works used by the author, and resources for readers who want to dig deeper into certain issues and subjects. It is intended to be more of a starting place than an exhaustive list. The page number or numbers in brackets after a listing indicates where in this text the work or author is referred to.

PRINT

Alterman, Eric. *What Liberal Media? The Truth about Bias and the News*. New York: Basic Books, 2003.

———. *Sound and Fury: The Making of the Punditocracy*. Ithaca, N.Y.: Cornell University Press, 2000.

Asimov, Isaac. *I, Robot*. New York: Gnome Press, 1950. [pages 88, 90] Asimov sets out the "Three Laws of Robotics."

Bloch, Marc. (1982). *Feudal Society: Social Classes and Political Organization*. Chicago: University of Chicago Press, 1982. [page 61]

Bollier, David. *Silent Theft: The Private Plunder of Our Common Wealth*. New York: Routledge, 2002.

Brock, David. *Blinded by the Right: The Conscience of an Ex-Conservative*. New York: Three Rivers Press, 2003. [page 155]

Dahl, Robert A. *How Democratic is the American Constitution?* New Haven, Conn.: Yale University Press, 2002. [page 157] "Dahl starts with the assumption that the legitimacy of the American Constitution derives solely from its utility as an instrument of democratic governance." (book jacket)

Drutman, Lee and Charlie Cray, *The Hidden Costs of War*. Cheney, Halliburton and the Spoils of War, session III, reading 1. Washington: Citizen Works, 2003. [page 44] From Citizen Works' Corporate Power Discussion Group. See http://www.citizenworks.org/corp/dg/s3r2.php.

Fuller, R. Buckminster. *Grunch of Giants*. New York: St. Martin's Press, 1983. [page 85] "Corporations are … socioeconomic ploys — legally enacted game-playing — agreed upon only between overwhelmingly powerful socioeconomic individuals and by them imposed upon human society and its all unwitting members." (excerpt)

Garofalo, Janeane, & Ben Stiller. *Feel This Book: An Essential Guide to Self-Empowerment, Spiritual Supremacy, and Sexual Satisfaction*. New York: Ballantine Books, 2000.

Harris, Bev. *Black Box Voting: Ballot Tampering in the 21st Century*. High Point, S.C.: Plan Nine Publishing, 2003. [page 117] "Harris exposes the shoddy programming, non-existent security and bald-faced lies that seem to dominate voting machine industry." (Amazon.com review)

Hartmann, Thom. *The Last Hours of Ancient Sunlight: Waking Up to Personal and Global Transformation*. New York: Three Rivers Press, 2000. [page 30] "Hartmann proposes that the only lasting solution to the crises we face is to re-learn the lessons our ancient ancestors knew—those which allowed them to live sustainably for hundreds of thousands of years" (book jacket)

———. *Unequal Protection: The Rise of Corporate Dominance and the Theft of Human Rights*. New York: Rodale Press, 2002. Gerry Spence (*Give Me Liberty*) says, "If we do not awaken soon, democracy will be replaced by a new 'Third Reich' of corporate tyranny. … No one has told us the truth better than Thom Hartmann. Read it!"

Hayden, Tom. *Irish on the Inside: In Search of the Soul of Irish America*. New York: Verso Books, 2003.

———. *Rebel: A Personal History of the 1960s*. Granada Hills, Calif.: Red Hen Press, 2003.

Herman, Edward S., & Chomsky, Noam. *Manufacturing Consent: The Political Economy of the Mass Media*. New York: Pantheon Books, 2002. [page 103] The authors "show that the news media … defend the economic, social, and political agendas of the privileged groups that dominate domestic society, the state, and the global order." (book jacket)

Hightower, Jim. *If the Gods Had Meant Us to Vote They Would Have Given Us Candidates*. New York: HarperCollins, 2000.

———. *Thieves in High Places: They've Stolen Our Country—And It's Time to Take It Back*. New York: Viking Press, 2003.

Korten, David. *The Post-Corporate World: Life After Capitalism*. San Francisco: Berrett-Koehler Publishers, 1999.

———. *When Corporations Rule the World*. San Francisco: Berrett-Koehler Publishers, 1995.

Madison, James. *Federalist #10: The Union as a Safeguard against Domestic Faction and Insurrection*. New York: The New York Packet, 1787. [page 158] The *Federalist Papers* is a series of 85 essays written by Alexander Hamilton, John Jay, and James Madison between October 1787 and May 1788. The essays explain particular provisions of the Constitution in detail and are often used to help interpret the intentions of those drafting the Constitution. Library of Congress: http://memory.loc.gov/const/fed/fedpapers.html.

McChesney, Robert W. and John Nichols, *Our Media, Not Theirs: The Democratic Struggle Against Corporate Media*, New York: Seven Stories Press, 2002. [page 104]

Orwell, George. *1984*. London: Secker & Warburg, 1949. [page 9]

Palast, Greg. *The Best Democracy Money Can Buy: The Truth About Corporate Cons, Globalization, and High-Finance Fraudsters*. New York: Plume, 2003. [page 123] Jim Hightower says, "The type of investigative reporter you don't see anymore—a cross between Sam Spade and Sherlock Holmes."

Phillips, Kevin. *The Emerging Republican Majority*. New Rochelle, N.Y.: Arlington House, 1969. [page 155] Phillips' prescient 1969 book predicted the takeover of the GOP by the ultraconservative fringe.

Pierce, William [Andrew Macdonald, pseud.], *The Turner Diaries*, Hillsboro, W. Va.: National Vanguard Press, 1978. [page 39]

Rand, Ayn. *Atlas Shrugged*. New York: Random House, 1957. [page 55] "The story of a society's slow collapse as the men of ability go on strike against the creed that treats them as sacrificial animals." (Ayn-Rand.com)

———. *The Fountainhead*. Indianapolis, Ind.: Bobbs-Merrill, 1943. [page 55] "Addresses a number of universal themes: the strength of the individual, the tug between good and evil, the threat of fascism." (Amazon.com review)

Ray, Paul H., & Sherry Ruth Anderson. *The Cultural Creatives: How 50 Million People Are Changing the World*. New York: Three Rivers Press, 2001. [page 163] Little-known, emergent progressive segment of the U.S. population interested in the Green Party, meditation, natural foods, exercise, holistic health, spirituality, and many other growing trends seeks balance and holism. (www.culturalcreatives.org.)

Williamson, Marianne. *Everyday Grace: Having Hope, Finding Forgiveness, and Making Miracles*. New York: Riverhead Books, 2002.

———. *Healing the Soul of America: Reclaiming Our Voices as Spiritual Citizens*. New York: Simon & Schuster, 2000.

VIDEO

Achbar, Mark (Producer & Director) and Wintonick, Peter (Director). *Manufacturing Consent: Noam Chomsky and the Media*. [VHS & DVD]. New York: Zeitgeist Films, 1992. [page 103] Available at www.zeitgeistfilms.com, "the documentary highlights Chomsky's probing analysis of mass media and his critique of the forces at work behind the daily news." (DVD jacket)

Greenwald, Robert (Producer & Director). *Uncovered: The Whole Truth about the Iraq War*. [VHS/DVD]. Culver City, CA: Carolina Productions, 2003. Interviews with more than 20 experts about the reasons we were given for war and the evidence presented to support those reasons. Available at www.truthuncovered.com

Perez, Richard Ray (Producer & Director), and Sekler, Joan (Producer & Director). *Unprecedented: The 2000 Presidential Election*. [VHS & DVD]. Santa Monica, Calif.: Alternavision Films, 2002. [page 123] A documentary about the battle for the Presidency in Florida and the undermining of democracy, available at www.unprecedented.org.

RADIO

For up-to-date information on Thom Hartmann's and other progressive radio programs (like Democracy Now), visit www.thomhartmann.com or www.we-the-people-book.com.

WORLD WIDE WEB

For up-to-date information on the topics in this book, check out:

> www.thomhartmann.com **Thom's site**.
> www.we-the-people-book.com **Official website of this book**.

AFL-CIO. www.aflcio.org. [page 130] Check this site for insight into what the unions of the American Federation of Labor and Congress of Industrial Organizations think about the conservative agenda.

Center for Voting and Democracy. www.fairvote.org. [page 161] Dedicated to fair elections. They build understanding of and support for more democratic voting systems and promote full representation as an alternative to winner-take-all elections, and instant run-off voting as an alternative to plurality elections and traditional run-off elections.

Citizens' Network on Essential Services. www.challengeglobalization.org. [page 49] Supports citizens' groups influencing policy decisions about basic services. Demystifies the roles of the World Bank, IMF. Great glossary of globalization terms and links to other sites.

Cultural Creatives. www.culturalcreatives.org. [page 163] This website is for the emergent, little-known progressive segment of the U.S. population that seeks balance and holism.

Code Pink. www.codepinkalert.org. [page 129] Code Pink is a women-initiated, grassroots, peace/social justice movement that seeks positive social change through proactive, creative protest, and non-violent direct action.

Democrats.com. www.democrats.com. [page 130] This site creates and implements effective Internet campaign services for Democratic campaigns and committees. There's more clarity, purpose, and political momentum on this activist-run site than on the Democratic Party's official website, www.democrats.org.

Drudge Report. www.drudgereport.com. [page 136] Journalist and gossipmonger Matt Drudge's conservative-leaning site posts links to breaking news stories by columnists like Ann Coulter, Rush Limbaugh and Drudge, himself.

Global Exchange. [page 49] http://www.globalexchange.org/. Provides education about democratizing the global economy. Seeks to strengthen the growing grassroots movement for ending corporate rule and furthering economic democratization. Lots of juicy ideas and links.

Global Policy Forum. www.globalpolicy.org. [page 49] Uses a holistic approach, linking peace and security with economic justice and human development, and places a heavy emphasis on networking to build broad coalitions for research, action, and advocacy. Lots of educational material

Innovations in Democracy. www.democracyinnovations.org. [page 129] A project of activist Tom Atlee's Co-Intelligence Institute that aims to make available hundreds of innovative practices, organizations, and other resources useful for building wiser democracies that work for all.

Judicial Watch. www.judicialwatch.org. [page 32] Non-partisan foundation that serves as an ethical and legal "watchdog" over our government, legal, and judicial systems to promote a return to ethics and morality in our nation's public life.

Landes, Lynn. www.ecotalk.org. [page 121] Investigative articles about politics, the environment, and more. Journalist Landes is one of the nation's foremost investigators of voting technology and democracy issues.

Mercuri, Rebecca. www.notablesoftware.com/evote.html. [page 121] Articles about electronic voting. Dr. Mercuri is a leading computer security and electronic vote tabulation specialist.

Public Citizen's Global Trade Watch. http://www.citizen.org/trade/. [page 49] Challenges corporate globalization, arguing that the current globalization model is neither a random inevitability nor "free trade." Makes the outcomes of globalization available to the public, press, and policy-makers. Excellent resources, including white papers, analyses, and a primer on globalization trade terms.

RadioPower.org Network. www.radiopower.org. [page 137] Streaming progressive talk radio with hosts Thom Hartmann, Marianne Williamson, and others. Provides links to progressive columnists, news services, periodicals, and more.

Raging Grannies (Seattle). www.ragingrannies.com. [page 129] Street theater activists dress up in outrageous hats and sing satirical songs to protest nuclear power, militarism, racism, clear-cut logging, and corporate greed.

The Scoop. www.scoop.co.nz. [page 123] Press-release-driven Internet news agency that delivers "disintermediated" news, leaving the reader to make the judgments. Scoop reported on disparities between poll and computer-controlled voting machine results.

Transformational Politics. www.transformationalpolitics.com. Explore the role of consciousness on our collective, consensual reality. Learn how to separate yourself from the seductive, polarizing influences of the mass mind.

UAW. www.uaw.org. [page 130] Find out what the United Automobile, Aerospace, and Agricultural Implement Workers of America International Union thinks about the conservative agenda.

Votewatch. www.votewatch.us. [page 115] Non-partisan group of citizen volunteers, statisticians, lawyers, technologists, journalists, and election officials who monitor public elections in the U.S., analyze patterns, and make their findings public prior to the certification

Undoing Corporate Personhood Law at State and Local Levels

Undoing corporate personhood will be a big task, but if you go to pages 294-326 of my book, *Unequal Protection*, you'll find guidance to get you started as well as model local ordinances and constitutional amendments that define persons as "natural persons" for each state. [Also check www.we-the-people-book.com]

In themselves, these actions will not overrule federal law, but they are a necessary step. Eventually, persistent action on this front will lead to two possibilities: Either the Supreme Court will reverse the duplicitous Santa Clara precedent in hearing the legal challenges that will surely follow, or there will be enough grassroots awareness and momentum to successfully promote a constitutional amendment. When a case challenging corporate personhood does reach the Supreme Court, we must hope that there is a majority of Justices who will honor both the Constitution and the Founders' intent enough to acknowledge the havoc wrought on the American political landscape by the Bellotti case and its reliance on the flawed Santa Clara headnote and will strip human rights from the non-humans entities. As several justices are nearing retirement, the 2004 presidential election takes on even more profound importance.

There is another approach worth looking at, as well.

Using a Non-binding Resolution to Educate Your Local Community

While passing a law to ban corporate personhood may seem the most direct way to take on the issue, it may not be the most rapid or the best for your community, at least in the beginning. First, it's necessary to educate a community, and passing a non-binding resolution (instead of a binding law or ordinance) can do just that. Although it won't have the force of law, it begins the process of change because proposing and campaigning for it will educate the voters in your community. The other benefit of passing a resolution is that it won't draw legal fire from corporations, who can challenge an ordinance and engage a community in costly litigation.

Beginning with a resolution as an educational effort, the process will almost certainly flow from the bottom up. As the issue becomes more and more visible, eventually either the Supreme Court will reverse their clerk's error of 1886 — the way in 1954 and 1973 they reversed their errors of 1896 and 1873, finally declaring that freed slaves and women are now "persons" under the law — or the States or Congress will take up the issue.

Whichever way the process of returning corporations to their former status ultimately happens, it'll only come about when a critical mass of the electorate realizes it's an issue.

A Case in Point

To that end, what the town of Point Arena, California, did in the year 2000 is an example of one of the most effective tools for educating people. Instead of passing an ordinance or law, the City Council passed a resolution declaring that the City of Point Arena didn't think corporations were persons.

The process took well over a year and was hotly debated in the town. As a result, today there is a high level of awareness about the corporate personhood issue in this part of northern California. Even thought the resolution didn't have the force of law, it was a tremendously successful educational process and, thus, may represent the best place for a local community to start.

Following is the text of the final draft of the resolution passed on a 4 to 1 vote by Point Arena's City Council on April 25, 2000.

RESOLUTION ON CORPORATE PERSONHOOD IN THE CITY OF POINT ARENA

Whereas,

- Citizens of the City of Point Arena hope to nurture and expand democracy in our community and our nation.
- Democracy means governance by the people. Only natural persons should be able to participate in the democratic process.
- Interference in the democratic process by corporations frequently usurps the rights of citizens to govern.
- Corporations are artificial entities separate and apart from natural persons. Corporations are not naturally endowed with consciousness or the rights of natural persons. Corporations are creations of law and are only permitted to do what is authorized under law.
- Rejecting the concept of corporate personhood will advance meaningful campaign finance reform.

Therefore be it hereby resolved that:

The City of Point Arena agrees with Supreme Court Justice Hugo Black in his 1938 opinion in which he stated, "I do not believe the word 'person' in the 14th Amendment includes corporations."

Be it further resolved that:

The City of Point Arena shall encourage public discussion on the role of corporations in public life and urge other cities to foster similar public discussion.

Thanks to Jan Edwards and Bill Meyers at The Community Environmental Legal Defense Fund (www.celdf.org) for permission to use the resolution here.

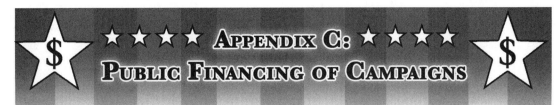

APPENDIX C:
PUBLIC FINANCING OF CAMPAIGNS

A problem seeking a solution

Consider the problem: According to the Center for Responsive Politics, in 1998, 96% of the contested Congressional races and 91% of the contested Senate races were won by the candidate who spent the most money.

Doesn't that suggest that something's wrong?

Even California's new Governor Schwarzenegger said it in one of his TV ads: "Special interests have a stranglehold on [California's capital] Sacramento. Here's how it works. Money comes in, favors go out. The people lose."

In Maine, three quarters of the state senators and half the state representatives ran "clean" — with only public funding and no private money.

In Arizona, 7 of the 9 statewide officeholders, including the present governor, ran clean. On her first day in office, Arizona Governor Janet Napolitano created a discount prescription drug program. Later, she reflected, "If I had not run clean, I would surely have been paid visits by numerous campaign contributors representing pharmaceutical interests and the like, urging me either to shelve that idea or to create it in their image, all the while ... wielding the implied threat to yank their support and shop for an opponent in four years."

Resources

To learn more about public financing of campaign expenses — the problem and the solution — here are some resources that could help:

www.publicampaign.org
Public Campaign
1320 19th Street N.W., Suite M-1
Washington, D.C. 20036
(202) 293-0222
e-mail: info@publicampaign.org
A wonderful resource for the "Clean Money, Clean Elections" movement.

www.campaignfinancesite.org
Great overview of history, current structure, court cases, legislation. A major feature is "Who's Giving to Whom." Follow the links and follow the money.

www.democracyctr.org
Look for "Campaign Financing — Agendas for Reform," from *The Democracy Owners Manual*

www.commoncause.org
Fair Elections SF has a good analysis of public financing from a San Francisco perspective.

www.commondreams.org
Search the site for articles on campaign financing.

www.capitalism.org
Capitalism Magazine's site presents the opposing view. Look for "'Campaign finance reform' is censorship masquerading as a solution for the problem of extortion by public officials."

www.we-the-people-book.com
This site posts updated resources and other information relevant to this book's topics.

THOM HARTMANN has authored over a dozen books, including two bestsellers and five books translated and published on four continents. His books have been reviewed in *Time* magazine. Businesses he has started have been featured on the front page of *The Wall Street Journal*. And he's been interviewed on numerous radio and TV shows, including NPR's *All Things Considered*, CNN and the BBC both for his writing and for his international relief work.

His book, *The Prophet's Way*, brought him a private audience with Pope John Paul II in 1998. The Dalai Lama was so impressed with *The Last Hours of Ancient Sunlight* that Hartmann spent a week with His Holiness in 1999.

Most recently, Hartmann began a syndicated radio talk show that reaches listeners across the country on terrestrial radio stations, the Sirius satellite radio system, and live on the Internet.

Thom is also the acclaimed creator of the "Hunter in a Farmer's World" metaphor for describing ADD and ADHD. His other recent books include *Unequal Protection: The Rise of Corporate Dominance and Theft of Human Rights* and *A Return To Democracy: Reviving Jefferson's Dream* (July, 2004).

Visit www.thomhartmann.com to keep up with his work, including free op-ed pieces.

NEIL COHN has recently been gaining attention for his research studying how the comic medium communicates, and has lectured on this topic in the United States and Europe. His artistic works have been featured in the textbook *Elementary Japanese*, and have inspired a ballet at the California Institute of the Arts.

Neil is the author of *Early Writings on Visual Language*, and his essays have appeared in several journals. He also serves as an advisor for CAST, Inc., a non-profit organization that develops technology for education.

Neil received an M.A. from the University of Chicago, a B.A. from the University of California, Berkeley, and has studied in Japan at Tsuru University. His next book will explore the cognition behind the comic book medium. You can find his work at www.emaki.net.

GENE LATIMER developed the idea for this book in March 2003 as his response to the political realities of our times. A veteran publisher and video producer, he co-creates media and events to accelerate spiritual awakening. You can follow his work on this as well as topics like quantum healing and radical "youthing" at www.tachyon-energy-products.com and www.christing.org (and through his free newsletters found there) — including The Christing Project, which he launched in 2006.

From his base in Portland, Oregon, Gene is currently developing shorter versions of the *We the People* book — with the same historical facts and framing and without a lot of the partisan elements — that are more suitable for classroom use (in both English and Spanish). Potential partners for that venture are welcome to contact him: gene@coreway.com.

PAUL W. BURKE Paul Burke has been writing seriously since he was ten years old. Since then, he's added editor, process facilitator and spiritual pilgrim to his résumé. In the 1990s he wrote for publications like *The Taos News* and Albuquerque's *Crosswinds Weekly*. He has an unpublished book, *Vanished Culture: Anasazi Exodus from the Colorado Plateau*, and two works in progress about movies as life's teachers and dreams of the culture. In 2005 he completed a three-year movie-based community dialogue program in Colorado Springs, Colorado, that explored human consciousness and meaningful life through series like the Mythology of War; (Re-) Emerging Feminine, Divine Feminine; the American Presidency; and Illusion and Reality.

At the beginning of 2006 he is planning to take the "Life, Meaning & Videotape" program on the road and expand his non-profit work. He can be reached at www.commonbridges.org.

ACKNOWLEDGEMENTS

Thom Hartmann:

I owe a special debt of gratitude to Craig Brown and the folks at CommonDreams.org who first published all of these articles, and to Gene Latimer for making this project into a reality and breathing it into life, to Paul Burke for so beautifully editing and blending my various articles into this book, and to Neil Cohn for his extraordinary artwork.

Neil Cohn:

Extensive thanks go to Gene Latimer and Thom Hartmann for trusting in me to venture into uncharted territory with this project, my brother Charlie and Ming Wong for their late night feedback and brainstorming, and my parents (Leigh and Lindsey) for their unending support and advice.

Paul Burke:

When Gene invited me to work on a book adaptation project, I had mixed emotions; I was anxious to get back to my own writing. Now, on the downhill slope, I see the absolute perfection of it all. Not only have I had the opportunity to do work that I love, I have also been blessed to work with a mature, sensitive and gifted Renaissance man who is a model of collaborative partnership. Thank you, Gene! And special thanks to my spiritual partner, Renée Brabant, for all her wisdom, insight and support on this project.

Gene Latimer:

This book has been a blessed project.

In the spring of 2003, I felt a deep need to get certain perspectives on what I saw unfolding in the United States out into print. For the previous six months, the most brilliant and compelling social commentator for me had been Thom Hartmann through his www.commondreams.org op-ed pieces. It felt critical to bring the forgotten and under-appreciated history of this country and the underlying political dynamics shaping current events — things that Thom articulates so well — to a wider audience. With that in mind, I approached him about weaving together two dozen of his articles into a single tapestry — all in a graphic format. Once he understood the concept, Thom was enthusiastically on board and has been a great joy to work with as we've transformed his words and perspectives into 187 comic pages.

After having searched literally for years — via job and Web postings and even want ads — for an illustrator to bring a substantive non-fiction book into form, the perfect person appeared at the perfect time. A couple of weeks before contacting Thom, I was speaking to an old friend about another matter when she made a tangential comment that her son was a comic book artist. Within three minutes of entering his website, I felt certain that Neil Cohn was the person I had been looking for. What extraordinary good fortune to find this skilled artist who possesses such an understanding of the nature of "visual language," such a passion for his craft and such dedication to serving the message through his chosen medium.

I embarked on this venture with little appreciation of the magnitude of the task of editing and restructuring 24 essays into a cohesive whole. Fortunately, I was inspired to recruit an old friend with whom I'd had little contact for the past decade to help me. It is challenging to adequately convey how invaluable Paul Burke's work, presence, and support have been in the successful completion of the book you hold. He's been a true godsend.

My heart-felt gratitude for whatever forces brought such a rewarding creative collaboration together.

Special mention must also be given to Jennifer Barker at CoreWay Media for her unwavering willingness to do whatever was needed and her diligent research, proofing and insightful feedback; and to Renée Brabant, who read the material multiple times, offering wise guidance. Likewise, Louise Hartmann has been wonderfully supportive through the entire process.

For reading the book at different stages and providing essential feedback, huge thanks to: David Korten, Eric Utne, Medea Benjamin, Lee Drutman, Steve Early, Michael Eisenscher, Robin Izer, Melissa Lippold, Franca Baroni, John Early, Heidi Sheppard, Gigi Rosenberg, Anne Kaplan, Sadie Faber, Linda and Alan Langhorn, Martin Fass, and Jesse Latimer. Numerous others have generously contributed critical, informative opinions regarding titles, subtitles and/or cover designs, including: Jimmie St. Arnold, Jenny Swanpool, Barbara Wilder, Robin Maynard-Dobbs, Carollyne MacLean, Greg Raymond, Cherie Staples, Lucia Thom, Gwendolyn Sharper, John Pacheco, Vimmy Khan, Kira Klatchko, Ken Faiman, Josh Lilienstein, Amy Flores, Mike Segal, and John Engstrom.

I am deeply grateful for the generous support of Lightsong and Bob Evans; for Jessica Sanders, Harald Hope and Jennifer Barker in enabling business to continue to function as the project moved forward; for Jesse and Cory Latimer being who they exquisitely are; and, especially, for Jane Latimer with whom I share my dance with Life.

INDEX

CoreWay Media

Accelerating Personal & Planetary Transformation

We the People ORDER FORM

Order *We the People* from your favorite bookseller if possible. Otherwise, you can order online, by mail, phone, or fax.

Pricing:

Per Copy: US$16.95
(US$4 total S&H in the United States, up to 7 copies)

Bulk Orders Per Copy: US$12.71
Receive a 25% discount on orders of 8 or more.
Purchase multiple copies for friends, family, your group or organization.
(US$5.98 total S&H for United States)

Special Carton Pricing Per Copy: US$10.16
Receive a 40% discount for 32 copies — that is, a full carton for $325!
(S&H is only $9.98 in the United States)

Online Orders: Place your order online at www.we-the-people-book.com

Mail Orders: Send your orders with payment to:
CoreWay Media, 3110 SE Arnold, Portland, OR 97219

Phone/Fax Orders: Phone: 888-200-8132, or fax the following form to 503-961-1553.

Name _____

Address _____

City _____ State _____ Zip _____

E-mail Address _____

Daytime Phone _____

Quantity _____   Payment Method (please circle):

Check   AMEX   Discover   MasterCard   Visa

Name on Card _____

Card # _____

Exp. Date _____